the WITHDRAWN

Improv Handbook

for

Modern Quilters

A Guide to Creating,

Quilting & Living Courageously

Sherri Lynn Wood

photography by sara remington

stc craft / a melanie falick book / new york

contents

Introduction

Almost twenty-five years ago I saw the exhibition *Who'd A Thought It* at the Ackland Art Museum at UNC-Chapel Hill, where I was living at the time. Organized by folklorist, collector, and Guggenheim Fellow Eli Leon, this was one of the first exhibitions of African-American quilts in the improvisational style to tour the country. Eli's breathtaking collection of quilts left me in awe and changed the course of my life. I began improvising in patchwork, which led to my professional career as an artist. Two years ago, just as I began work on *The Improv Handbook,* I met Eli Leon at a presentation I was giving to the East Bay Modern Quilt Guild. We became friends. We now visit regularly, usually at his home, where he gives me full access to his collection. We discuss the aesthetic qualities and the stories behind the quilts and their makers. I've been given an incredible opportunity to incorporate some of Eli's brilliant research along with my experiential knowledge of improvisatory practice into this practical guide for modern quilters.

Improvisation is at the heart of every great creative endeavor. Music, dance, theater, painting, drawing, design, cooking, conversation, relationships, play, life, and even science benefit, survive, grow, transform, and innovate through the flexibility of mind that the improvisational process engenders. We all improvise every day, so why not bring it into our quilt making?

Eli put the whole matter so clearly in an essay published in 2006 by Figge Art Museum, Davenport, Iowa, in a catalogue based on the exhibit *Accidentally on Purpose.* "When a flexible pattern is handed on from one quiltmaker to another it is the range of possibilities that is transmitted." And that's my goal for this book; to hand to you flexible patterns, called scores, so that you may discover your range of improvisatory possibilities.

The Improv Handbook offers a unique approach to patchwork that doesn't rely on step-by-step instructions for replicating fixed patterns. Instead it provides frameworks, or scores, for flexible patterning that support improvisatory exploration. It also includes a comprehensive set of tools that will empower you to move beyond beginner-level improv to create with an authentic voice, speaking what is genuine and real to you, in a voice that is not copied or false.

Throughout you'll find scores to follow that explore approaches and methods from different improvisational disciplines. As you follow each score, you'll set limits to your improvisation and create a quilt based on those limits. With each score you'll find Design Consideration sidebars with design concepts and exercises for you to consider as you follow any of the scores in the book. The Mind Tool sidebars offer exercises for fostering fearlessness, presence, and curiosity as you embark on your improvisational journey.

While each score builds on the previous ones, the information flows forward and backward throughout the book. You will be asked to build on techniques learned for earlier scores or referred back to a particularly apt Design Consideration sidebar. If you are a beginner, you may want to start with Score #1 and work your way through the scores in the order they are given. Otherwise, jump in according to your skill level and improvisational experience and what is most appealing for you to explore. You may even want to begin with the chapter on improvisational patchwork techniques, which starts on page 120.

If you picked up this handbook to learn how to make quilts that look like mine, I'm sorry to disappoint. I can't teach you how to do that. I can't even replicate my own quilts, because each one is unique to the moment it was made. But I can help you hone your improvisational skills. In the gallery after each score you can see how contributors interpreted it. Now it is your turn.

My hope is that you will approach each score as an opportunity for discovery and pleasure. The goal is to have fun and learn from everything you do and from every quilt you make. Take each quilt as a beacon guiding you ever closer to knowing your own patterns and clarifying your authentic voice. Let's begin!

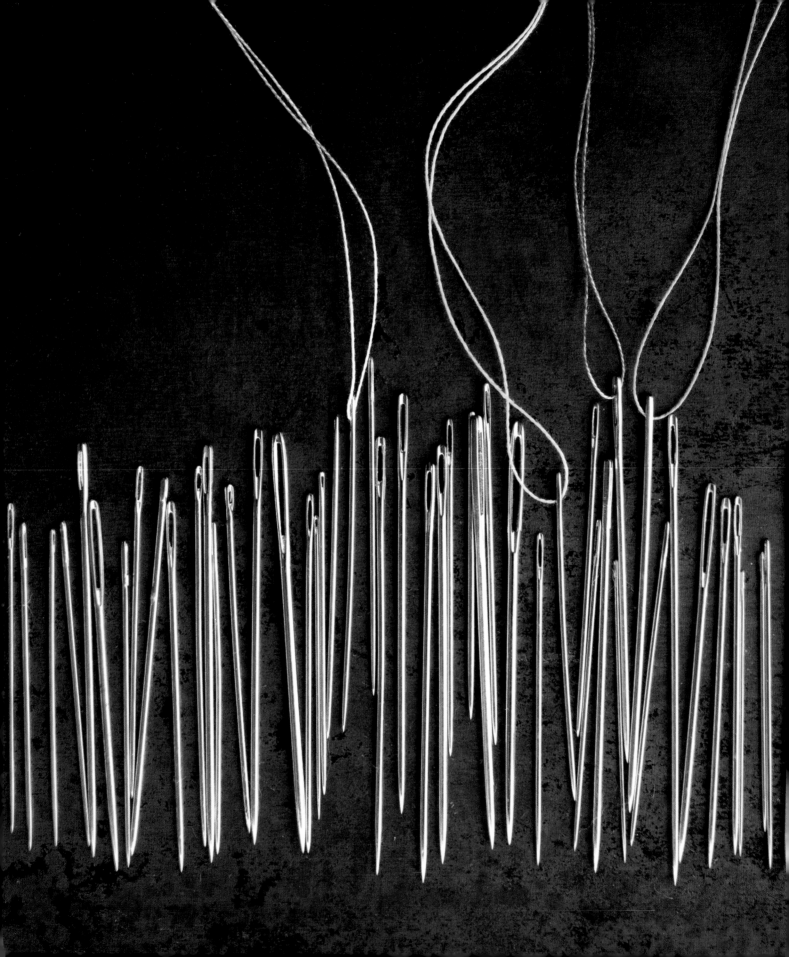

1

Improvising
From a Score

What Is Improv?

Before reading further, take a few minutes to brainstorm what "improv" means to you right now.

Whenever I teach an improvisational patchwork class, I ask my students this question and am always delighted by the array of answers I receive (see right).

What resonates with you as you read this list? What would you like to add to it? Is there anything unexpected on this list? Anything you disagree with?

You may be wondering why I am asking you to ponder all these questions instead of just telling you what improv is all about. The answer is because improvisation is about exploring, not explaining. It's about finding your own way and making your own decisions through noticing your own preferences and patterns of mind.

In this chapter, I share the things you need to prepare for your improvisational patchwork journey, and I describe a bit more the vehicle for the journey: the score.

working without a plan!

thinking on your feet!

figuring out as you go!

making do with what you have!

problem-solving!

taking risks!

breaking the rules!

decision-making!

anything goes!

accepting what is!

creating spontaneously!

freedom and responsibility!

freedom from perfection!

setting your own limits!

Preparing to Improvise

Developing an improvisatory patchwork practice requires a rethinking of all aspects of the craft, including basic understandings about the flexible use of tools as well as fabric, workspace, techniques, color, design, and pattern. Nothing is fixed. Before beginning, pause here to reconsider everything you know about the basics of quilt making.

Tools are designed to function well when used a particular way, but that doesn't mean they can't be improvised to do something different or new. The table knife was designed to cut food, but sometimes I use the handle to bang on the stuck lid of a jar to loosen it. If you have to get something done, use whatever tools you have available, in any way possible, to achieve the results you desire.

Get to know all your tools well, from your sewing machine to your pins. What can you make them do? How comfortable are you using them and in what circumstances? Some people, for instance, feel unsafe using a rotary cutter without a ruler; if that's the case for you, try using scissors. Or practice becoming more comfortable safely using the rotary cutter on its own. Become so familiar with your tools that they become an extension of you, just as the musician's instrument is an extension of her voice.

SEWING MACHINE: Keep your sewing machine in great working order, well oiled and serviced. Let it hum and be a joy to work with. Establishing a happy, trusting relationship with your machine will keep frustration at bay, support your efforts to explore new techniques, and increase your willingness to attempt tricky piecing situations as they arise.

PRECISION TOOLS: Set aside your rulers and templates as you work through the project scores in this book. All of the cutting you'll do will be by your own hand, guided by expression rather than a ruler. It sounds scary, but it really does make sense when you're improvising. See my top five reasons to go ruler-free at left.

CUTTING TOOLS: Scissors vs. rotary cutter? Try and experiment with both. Each will yield different aesthetic outcomes and can be more or less useful depending on the piecing situation at hand. Get comfortable using them interchangeably. Don't forget the handy seam ripper; it's a clever little tool to have nearby.

PINS AND MARKING TOOLS: To pin or not to pin? Even the way you pin will affect your outcome. How you use your tools and when you use them is not to be taken for granted, even when it comes down to the simplest rote details of marking and pinning. I share how I use chalk and pins to mark and match seam lines on pages 136–137, but test it out for yourself and see what works for you.

TOP 5 REASONS TO GO RULER-FREE

5

Precise measurement vectors energy away from improvisational flow. Going ruler-free supports spontaneity and play.

4

Mechanical, ruler-made lines always communicate the same thing. A freely cut line can convey your personality and a variety of expressions, just as a hand-drawn line or your signature can.

3

Patchwork construction becomes less familiar without the habit of templates to depend on, leading to a deeper understanding of how patterns work. Responding to happy accidents adds beauty and interest to your quilts.

2

You become the measure of things and will grow to trust your own authority. Get used to being the ruler instead of depending on one.

1

You don't need a ruler to make your pieces fit together and lie flat. Your hand-eye coordination will improve. Soon enough you will be able to cut perfect 1" (2.5-cm) strips without a ruler if you want to.

PRESSING TOOLS: The iron is an essential tool. If you don't have one you love, ditch it and find a new pressing mate. The two of you will be spending a lot of time together.

I press on a padded board with a lot of steam from my gravity-feed iron, a heavy, industrial iron with a large water reservoir that can put out a lot of heat and steam. Whatever iron you prefer, make sure it has steam functionality. Sometimes I hover the iron above my seams and steam them until they begin to soften and bend toward their natural inclination before heavy pressing. Sometimes I press in one direction or from the center out. Sometimes I start pressing on the wrong side, sometimes on the right side. I press in the manner most suited to my desired outcome or most suited to what the material wants. There is no one right way to press.

OTHER TOOLS: Enlist other tools around the house or invent new ones to meet your needs. For example, I regularly use blue painter's tape to mark the target shape of my quilt when I'm building up my composition arrangement on the floor.

FABRICS

The first, and often one of the most inspiring, step in making any quilt is choosing the fabrics. When creating a planned quilt, it is standard practice to choose just the right amount of fabric for the entire quilt before the patchwork begins. When improvising, the process of choosing fabrics is more organic and will evolve throughout the quilt-making process.

Finished sizes and fabric amounts for the quilts are not specified since it will be up to you to determine the size of your quilt. When I begin a project, I sometimes "audition" fabrics on my design wall. I spread them out to see how their colors, values, and patterns work together. I also note their coverage on the wall in relationship to the target quilt size. In this way, I determine the approximate amounts needed.

Once I get an idea of the range of fabrics and the amounts I might need, I curate the fabrics a bit more depending on the limits I set for the project. If I have a large piece of yellow,

HAND-PIECING TOOLS: Never leave home without them. When you are improvising, you always want to be prepared. Tricky piecing situations requiring hand stitching can arise at any time. I keep a variety of both appliqué and embroidery needles in my sewing kit.

If I had to choose one color of sewing thread, it would be medium gray. It blends the best for sewing a full range of values and colors by hand or by machine.

Thimbles are a personal preference, and there's quite a range from which to choose. I use a recessed metal thimble on the middle finger of my sewing hand. If your fingertips are sensitive, find one that works best for you. Soon your thimble will feel like a second skin.

See the finishing techniques on page 154 for more information on thread and needle options for hand quilting.

let's say a yard (1 m), but I want to limit myself to using only a small amount of yellow, I will cut the yard down to, let's say, ¼ yard (.25 m) and store the rest away. Curating fabrics in this way is not an exact calculation. If you come up short on a fabric during the course of the improvisation, it's a lucky opportunity to make a substitution. (See Making Do on page 67.)

Any material you have on hand that can be sewn can be used in a quilt. The important part is to have it on hand. Improvisation will take unexpected turns, so any fabric visible in your workspace has the potential to end up in your quilt.

Selvage-to-selvage yardage is useful for strip piecing, for making bias strips, or when featuring a large amount of one fabric in a composition.

Scraps, both small and large, can be used to make an entire quilt or spontaneously mixed in with a curated group of fabrics as filler and substitutions. You never know when a scrap will come in handy to perk up your quilt and process at just the right moment. I organize scraps by size and sometimes by component. I keep precut selvage-to-selvage strips, bias strips, curve pieces, triangles, and pieced scraps separate from general bits and pieces of small to large scraps.

The types of fabrics used in a quilt will affect its tone. Let's look at some types of fabrics and their properties according to the way I understand them in my own work.

× Commercial solids operate like paint. They are pure color, devoid of any other association. They allow the eye to rest when used with lots of prints. They are flat and have a Pop Art feel.

× Hand-dyed solids also operate like paint but with slightly more texture. They have more complexity and depth than commercial solids for a more artisan tone.

× Commercial prints operate like collage. Each connotes a particular style, narrative, visual texture, scale, identifiable historical era, and, sometimes, culture. Prints will excite the eye if used with mostly solids.

× Stripes, plaids, and dots operate like paint and collage. They add visual texture and scale, and they direct the eye.

× Monotone prints and batiks are more like prints than solids. They carry subtle texture and style. They focus attention on color but do not allow the eye to rest as solids do.

× Non-cottons add texture. Their surfaces direct light.

× Recycled/up-cycled clothing can carry personal narratives and trigger memory.

As you improvise, pay attention to how different types of fabrics operate in your quilts. Notice your habits of choice, and challenge yourself to push past your preferences to explore new territory.

OUTER SPACE / *THE STUDIO*

Your studio environment will affect the outcome of your quilts. If you don't have a designated creative workspace in your home, do what you can to commandeer a part-time space or rent a studio outside the home with your local quilting group. Convert a shed, or move a vintage trailer into your backyard. One way or another, you deserve space in which to create.

The vertical space of a design wall is handy for viewing your patchwork as it evolves. Create a portable design wall by simply tacking or taping a sheet of batting, flannel, or felt on an empty wall or door to arrange your patchwork on. When you are done for the day, just roll your patchwork up in the sheet and store it away until your next session. If you are able, install a permanent design wall by attaching sheets of insulation board, which will accept a pin without bending it, to your wall and covering it with flannel or felt.

Horizontal space, such as a floor, a large table, or the top of a bed, will allow you to move pieces around easily and to build your quilts in the round. Improvise and use the features available to you in your workspace. For example, if you have linoleum tiles or hardwood floorboards, use them as measuring guides for squaring off finished quilt tops.

Sometimes space is limited and there is nothing to be done but to "make do" with less than the ideal. If you have little or no horizontal and/or vertical space, don't let that stop you from improvising. Go ahead and piece your sections and build your quilt without being able to view it as a whole. It will be fabulous.

INNER SPACE / *NURTURING AN IMPROVISATIONAL MIND*

Not only is it essential to prepare the physical space of the studio, it's equally as important to nurture the inner space and improvisatory attitude of the mind. Growing your capacity for curiosity, courage, risk-taking, flexibility, and acceptance is essential for improvising, even more so than mastering techniques or learning new methods of improvisation. That is why there are Mind Tool sidebars throughout the book. Use them to develop your inner skills for improvisation, just as you would improvisational sewing techniques, to develop physical skills and design exercises to develop aesthetic skills. Your mind is a muscle, and it needs to be exercised!

The Mind Tools are scattered throughout the project chapters, but feel free to apply them whenever you are improvising, as needed. It is important to make the Mind Tools your own. Try them the way they are written. If they work for you, great; if not, adapt them to fit your needs.

IN-BETWEEN SPACE / *THE SKETCHBOOK/JOURNAL*

The sketchbook/journal is a place for creative pondering in words and through images and is the bridge between inner and outer space. It is the place to write thoughts and observations, evaluate process and outcomes, reflect on aesthetic as well as personal discoveries, sketch ideas, and develop new projects. I recommend designating a special blank book to be *your* own

TECHNIQUES

Improv has its own set of techniques and skills. Years ago at my local quilt guild, a guest speaker presented an image of an amazing improvisational quilt, with all its intelligent imperfections and flexible patterning, and quipped, "This quilter must have gotten up on the wrong side of the bed the day she made this!" Everyone laughed, but I recognized that this brilliant quilt maker was not fuzzy-headed and confused. She had deftly employed a different set of skills to achieve a different set of aesthetic goals in her improvisational work at a time when precision patchwork was recognized as the only standard for "well-made" quilts.

You will find a comprehensive set of improvisational patchwork techniques, from basic to advanced, starting on page 120. These techniques can be applied as needed to resolve whatever piecing situations may arise. If you're an experienced seamstress and/or quilt maker, add to these any and all sewing techniques you've ever learned. Employ, adapt, and innovate with your full range of knowledge. If you don't know how to do something, make up a way. Anything goes to get the job done. If you've never sewn or quilted in your life, your beginner's mind will work to your advantage. Because you are a beginner and have few preconceptions about processes or techniques, you'll likely be open to trying and experimenting. Sewing isn't that hard. Jump right in.

YOU

You are actually the most important aspect of improvisation. You have to show up. You have to be present. You have to know your likes and dislikes. You have to be responsive to your choices. You have to feel your emotions. You have to be whole to yourself in a non-judgmental and accepting way. Nothing more and nothing less will make your quilts sing.

Harnessing your emotional energy by being present to what you are feeling while you are creating is the key to developing your improvisatory range and authentic voice. Listen to John Coltrane's "In a Sentimental Mood" and you will know exactly what I mean.

improv handbook as a companion that completes this *Improv Handbook*. I am not the only writer here. There are clear cues scattered throughout this handbook for brainstorming, doodling, evaluating, setting limits, sketching, noting color inspiration, and adapting and even writing scores. Only your journal can complete *The Improv Handbook* so that it becomes a definitive reference for you.

TIME

Make time to improvise. Do what you need to do to work without distraction. When possible, turn off your cell phone, and place a Do Not Disturb sign on your workroom door. The Centering Exercise on page 47 is designed to help you clear the decks so that you can access your creative flow.

The Score

Now that you are prepared to improvise, let's explore the vehicle for learning how to improvise used in this book: the score.

In creating a musical score, a composer is making a record of how the music is to be performed. Yet each performance of the score will be unique. Even classically notated scores are open to a certain amount of interpretation by the conductor and orchestra. With jazz music, the score (called a lead sheet) has room for a wider interpretation. A jazz score will capture the essential elements of a composition without specifying details. It is used to give basic indications of melodies, chord changes, and arrangements, while providing room for unique interpretations and unrepeatable variations.

Think of a traditional block pattern as a classical music score. There is room for some variation in tone or momentum, but the notes of a classical score are followed rather precisely. When you create a quilt based on a traditional block pattern, you may choose your own colors and fabrics, change the scale of the block, and set the blocks differently or with sashing, but the overall range of variation is relatively limited.

Now imagine designing a quilt in a way that is like following a jazz lead sheet.

If you think there are no rules in improvisation, allow me to dispel that misconception. There are rules or limits, but they can be broken, pushed, or redefined at any time.

Limits can be fertile ground for innovation. The Gee's Bend quilts were created by a group of women who lived in the isolated African-American hamlet of Gee's Bend, Alabama. They had very few resources and had no choice but to "make do" in life and in their quilt making. The material limits they faced on a daily basis required innovation. Their quilts reflect their inventive intelligence and abundant spirit for overcoming these limits. Their brilliant improvisational approaches to composition, more often associated with twentieth-century abstract painters, received critical acclaim when their quilts were discovered and exhibited at the Whitney Museum of American Art in 2002. The quilts of Gee's Bend have inspired a whole new generation of artists and quilt makers alike.

BRAINSTORMING LIMITS FOR PATCHWORK

Let's look at some limits you could use to create an improvisational patchwork score:

TIME
Make a quilt top in two hours.

MATERIAL AMOUNTS
Precut the quantities of materials and use everything.

TYPES OF MATERIALS
Use only solids, or use only plaids and stripes.

SHAPE
Use only squares or strips or triangles or strips with triangles.

SCALE/SIZE
Use only strips 1" to 3" (2.5 cm to 7.5 cm) wide.

COLOR
Use strips in warm colors and squares in cool colors. (See page 112 for more on color.)

PROCEDURAL
Whenever one limit (such as shape) is used, another limit (such as size or color) must follow. For example, you might decide that sections of square shapes must be joined with black or white strips.

CHANCE
Ask five friends to independently send you a piece of fabric that must be used in your quilt, or choose strips randomly from a bag of mixed colors.

••

What other limits can you imagine setting for your patchwork? What limits might be most challenging for you? What limits may nurture a sense of safety and freedom for you? Why? Take a moment to consider your responses and write them down.

CREATING YOUR OWN SCORE

The scores for my projects usually evolve organically. Sometimes I begin by choosing the colors, then I consider the amount of each color I want to use and the shapes and patterns I want to explore. After I patch together a few sections, I play around with them until a composition begins to take shape. The direction of the composition often shifts as I pause and visually attend to each decision I commit to along the way. Sometimes I start with a general vision for the composition, but I never hold onto it too tightly.

For this book, I've written out my scores so that I can share them with you. Here are some tips for creating and refining your own scores:

✖ Complete the brainstorming exercise described on page 19. Select three limits from your list and write out your own score for an improvised quilt. Ideas for other limits can be saved for another quilt or used to further define this one, if desired.

✖ After you have made a quilt from your original score, ask a quilting buddy or your quilting circle to improvise quilts based on your original score before they see your version. When their interpretations are complete, look at all the quilts together and do the Evaluation Exercise at right.

✖ Work in a series by performing or improvising your score more than once. After each improvisation, use the Evaluation Exercise at right to tweak and change the limits of your score for different results.

mind tool
EVALUATION EXERCISE

Never judge a work as good or bad. Instead, here is a simple exercise for evaluating your work in a non-judgmental way. I use this to evaluate both my process and my finished quilts and to determine my next steps. Write down your responses during and/or at the completion of each project score.

What surprised me?

What did I discover or learn?

What was satisfying about
the process or outcome?

What was dissatisfying?

If dissatisfied, what can I do differently
next time to be more satisfied?

Where do I want to go from here?

2

Quilt Scores

Improv Is . . .
Setting Limits to Expand Horizons
·· floating squares ··

It may seem like a paradox, but limits have the ability to take us off the beaten path and expand our horizons in unexpected ways.

> Have you ever suffered a broken heart only to realize that your capacity for love had increased? Or battled a severe illness that kindled your sense of gratitude? Or experienced the death of a friend or family member that awakened your willingness to forgive? Sometimes limits are forced on us, and our human spirit makes something beautiful out of the hardship. But we also have the ability to identify and define limits for ourselves that allow us to survive, thrive, and transform. In fact, setting limits provides a safe container for risk-taking.

As you tailor the limits for each of the project scores in this book, pay attention to the threshold where safety and freedom meet for you. If you become immobilized by too many choices, try narrowing the limits of the score so you feel more comfortable. If your creative flow feels restricted, widen the limits of the score. If you find yourself stuck in a habitual pattern, become a pioneer. Tailor your limits in a way that challenges you to explore unknown territory with an edge of confidence. Explore this dynamic through your patchwork as you practice it in your life and relationships.

Score for Floating Squares

Perhaps my most basic improvisational patchwork score, Floating Squares is deceptively simple. But don't be fooled: There are many opportunities for play. Once you get the hang of this score, you can easily piece a quilt in a day—and you may very well end up making five variations in five days.

If you have never improvised with patchwork, this is a great place to begin. Floating Squares provides a clear model for how to work from a score rather than from a prescribed pattern. This score provides an opportunity to explore the design element of scale and introduces two beginning-level improv techniques: Equalizing Patchwork Sections (page 122) and Ruler-Free Patchwork (page 124).

For this score, you set the limits for fabric amounts and the scale or size of squares, and you define a process for carrying out the patchwork. I provide specific examples of limits and choices. But by setting your own limits and making your own choices, you will discover exciting new territories of creative expression.

Remember that the score and the limits you set are the starting point. At any time you may choose to remain true to the score, or you may choose to alter limits and adapt the score.

step 1. choose a limited group and amount of fabrics

Begin by choosing three fabrics. Choose a limited amount of two of the fabrics. The limited amount you choose for these fabrics can vary or be the same. You will also need an unlimited amount of the third fabric, which will be used as a "filler fabric" to fill in empty spaces. There is no way to tell how much filler fabric you will need at this time. But don't worry if you run out; you can always substitute a new filler fabric. For more help with curating fabrics and choosing amounts, see page 14.

step 2. choose limited sizes for your squares

Precut the two fabrics of limited quantity into a range of different-sized squares without using a ruler. The squares do not have to match or have even sides or 90° angles. Decide on the size range for each of the first two fabrics. For example, you may cut the first fabric into squares that range in size from 2" to 4" (5 cm to 10 cm) and the second fabric into squares that range in size from 4" to 6" (10 cm to 15 cm). The size range of your squares will affect the outcome of your composition. (See Exploring Scale on page 28.) No need to cut up the filler fabric at this stage.

step 3. choose a patchwork process

Sew the different-sized precut squares together. It is easy to join the precut squares of different sizes by equalizing the length of the squares or patchwork units and adding in small filler fabric strips and rectangles as needed. See Equalizing Patchwork Sections on page 122.

In this way, squares become units and units grow into sections. Continue to build in this manner until all the squares have been sewn together or you have reached the target size of your quilt. Use as much filler fabric as you need to do this. If you run out of filler fabric or squares, substitute other fabrics. For more about fabric substitutions see Making Do on page 67.

As your units get larger, refer to the technique Ruler-Free Patchwork on page 124 to join sections with different-shaped edges (but already of equal length) without a ruler or template.

step 4. evaluate your experience and results

Apply the Evaluation Exercise (page 20), after making your quilt top to assess what you've learned from the experience and to identify what you might like to do differently next time.

SCORE #1 ADAPTATIONS

As you work on Floating Squares, most likely your process will flow naturally without too much thought. At some point you may begin to notice there are multiple options for how to proceed. Limit and define your process if you need more structure. Switch to a different set of choices and limitations if you are less than satisfied with the way your composition is evolving. I tend to mix and match my approaches; here are just a few possibilities:

- ✖ Start by sewing together only squares that contrast with each other. Sew very large squares to very small squares. As they gradually equalize in size, you will be using less filler fabric.

- ✖ Join all your squares making units of just two squares and filler fabric. Then sew the units to each other using the filler fabric. Continue this way until you have built one big section.

- ✖ Join two squares and add that unit to another square with filler fabric to create larger and larger units.

You can also adapt the score in other ways:

- ✖ Change the hue and/or values of your fabrics.

- ✖ Use stripes and/or plaids cut off-center for your squares and/or filler fabric.

- ✖ Work with only three sets of squares and one filler fabric.

- ✖ Vary the scale of precut squares. See Exploring Scale, right.

- ✖ Cut your squares wonky, slightly off square.

- ✖ Set a tight time limit to encourage more spontaneity.

- ✖ Work with a different shape; for example, precut your fabrics into triangles instead of squares.

- ✖ Work in the round, building outward from the center in all directions.

- ✖ Combine more than one colorway set of Floating Squares in a single composition.

- ✖ Devise other ways can you push the limits of this score.

As your composition grows, you may find these additional techniques helpful.

Ruler-Free Patchwork with Large Sections: Use when the sections being joined are larger than your rotary mat, page 130.

Darting: Troubleshooting technique for taking out wobbles when the patchwork doesn't lie flat, page 128.

Natural Shaping: Tips for trimming your sections before joining, page 134.

Patchwork Puzzle: Composition tips, page 134.

---

design consideration
EXPLORING SCALE

Good design includes the ability to make interesting shifts in scale. Use the score for Floating Squares to practice moving from small to large squares and from a lesser to greater range of size disparity between squares.

- ✖ Following the score, create a series of sections beginning with small-sized squares with a 2" (5-cm) range: 1"–3" (2.5 cm–7.5 cm), for example.

- ✖ Next move to medium-sized squares with a 3" (7.5-cm) range: 3"–6" (7.5 cm–15 cm).

- ✖ Move to larger size squares with a 4" (10-cm) range: 6"–10" (15 cm–25 cm).

  You can continue playing with scale in this way by setting your own parameters for square size and range with each new section, such as 5"–7" (13 cm–18 cm), 3"–9" (7.5 cm–23 cm), or 1"–10" (2.5 cm–25 cm).

- ✖ If you are into math, you might figure out a way to use the Fibonacci sequence (1, 1, 2, 3, 5, 8, 13, 21 . . .) to set parameters for the size and range of your squares!

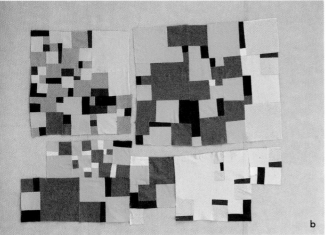

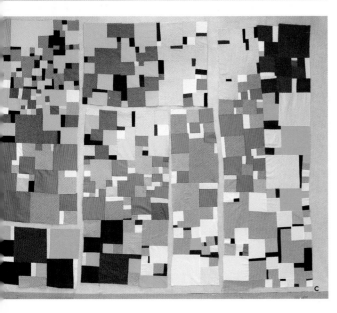

AS I BEGAN MAKING my Floating Squares quilt (page 24) I had no idea that the algorithmic process would result in something that looked so digital. I also discovered, after staring at this quilt for a while, that the perceptual phenomenon of afterimage colors (page 117) actually appears, adding another layer of complexity. I am very satisfied with the outcome!

SCORE ADAPTATION: I worked multiple sections of the basic score in different colorways. Each section was built up to fit onto the previous section(s). When all the sections were complete I then combined them into a single composition.

FABRICS: For each colorway section I paired afterimage colors of solid fabrics for my precut squares and used either a light or dark neutral solid for the filler fabric. For example, in one section I paired orange and turquoise and used a deep blue for filler fabric. **(a)**

SIZE: In each section I also varied the size of my precut squares. The range of square sizes was consistent in both precut colors within each section, but from section to section, I increased the size of the squares. In the first section, in the top left corner of the quilt, the precut squares for both fabrics ranged from 2" to 4" (5 cm to 10 cm) with a few larger squares, up to 9" (23 cm). Later sections included squares that ranged in size from 5" to 11" (13 cm to 28 cm). **(b)**

PROCESS: I built multiple medium-sized units in each colorway with the goal of using all of my precut squares. I then shifted them around on a design wall and joined the colorways into larger units. To equalize seam lengths and blend the large sections, I sometimes cut squares to fit the empty spaces to avoid long, visually dividing strips of filler fabric. **(c)**

SCORE #1: Floating Squares

score #1

·· floating squares ··

Ashley Newcomb (far right) and Emily Cummings (near right, bottom) both followed the basic score for Floating Squares faithfully, using only three fabrics. Ashley chose a white filler fabric that blends with the blue polka dot, which causes the pale gray squares to show up for a subtle low-impact effect.

In Emily's interpretation, the intense blue filler fabric takes center stage when employed against neutral gray and black squares.

Michelle McLatchy's score adaptation (near right, top) reflects several rounds of square combinations. She shifted the relationship of value between her squares with each new round but used the same white filler fabric to create a scattered yet unifying field of negative space.

Michelle McLatchy   Ashley Newcomb
Emily Cummings

Improv Is . . . Doing It My Way

·· strings ··

Improvisation is all about freedom of choice. But the responsibility that comes with freedom of choice may make you feel uncertain. Perhaps you don't like not being able to see where your decisions will lead. Or maybe you don't trust yourself to make the "right" decisions. But with each decision you make, you are a step closer to doing things your own unique way.

Improvisational patchwork is an opportunity to discover and know your own mind. Becoming aware of your likes and dislikes leads to confident and spontaneous decision-making. Noticing preferences is an opportunity to discover your habits, which in turn allows you to see the fork in the road leading to new territory.

Score for Strings

Ruler-Free Strip Piecing (page 127) is a foundation-building technique. Foundations are pieced from scraps, or in this case strips, to create another fabric that you can later cut into specific shapes as you would any piece of fabric bought off the bolt. Piecing long strips of fabric together makes a beautiful foundation fabric, which I call a string sheet, suitable for use in home and fashion items as well as in quilt making. String sheets can be cut into a pattern to make a tote bag, used as the border on a set of curtains, or cut into triangles to create a flying geese quilt.

This score also introduces the technique of Cutting from Your Core (page 126), which is the key to creating expressive string sheets and tapping into your signature line when cutting ruler-free.

step 1. curate your fabrics

Choose three distinctive but related sets of fabrics to cut into strips for your string sheets using large scraps or selvage-to-selvage yardage. Make the string sheets large enough to meet the target size of your quilt. You'll have two options for composing with them. For the first option, you'll need yardage of a neutral fabric to use as a filler fabric or to create negative space. For the second option, you'll need dark and light single strips for joining your string-pieced sheets.

step 2. set limits for your string sheets

Set limits to create three distinctive string sheets. The possibilities are unlimited. Decide what limits you are most interested in exploring and start simple. You don't need to vary the limits for every attribute in every set.

STRIP WIDTH: Use only narrow 1" to 1½" (2.5 cm to 4 cm) strips in one set, 2" to 4" (5 cm to 10 cm) strips in another set, and a range of 1" to 5" (2.5 cm to 13 cm) strips in the third.

PRINT AND/OR SOLIDS: Alternate solids and prints in one set, use only stripes and solids in another set, and use all solids in a third set.

NUMBER OF DIFFERENT FABRICS IN EACH STRING SHEET: Use two fabrics, like white and black, or use ten different fabrics in a single string sheet.

RANGE OF COLOR: Use yellows for one set, blues for another set, and yellows and blues for the third.

RANGE OF VALUE: Have one set be high contrast with a wide range of values, one set low impact in the light range of values, and another set low impact in a dark set of values. See more on color on page 112.

step 3. cut your strips from your core

Begin by cutting strips without a ruler to match the limits you have set. Everyone has a signature way of writing or drawing; it's no different when cutting freehand. Your signature line will fall somewhere on the continuum between wavy and straight. You can cut your strips with a rotary cutter or a scissors by following the technique for Cutting From Your Core on page 126.

step 4. sew your string sheets rhythmically

Set a sequence for your sewing order and define your selection methods, such as always following a light-valued strip with a dark-valued strip. You may also want to apply these selection methods to your sequence.

RANDOM: Put all your strips in a single set in a bag and choose them randomly.

SPONTANEOUS: Quickly choose one strip at a time as you sew.

PLANNED: Lay out twenty strips in the order you want to sew them and stick to your plan as you sew.

BATCHED: Quickly choose and sew two strips together and repeat five to ten times. Then sew two sets of pairs together and

repeat until all the pairs are sewn. Then sew the quads together and so on until all strips are sewn into one string sheet.

Once you have your process defined, sew the strips following the technique for Ruler-Free Strip Piecing on page 127. Apply the Evaluation Exercise on page 20 and note your discoveries. Which process did you enjoy more? Are there noticeable differences in the outcomes? Which selection method produced the best strip sets?

step 5. compose your quilt with the string sheets

Now that you have created at least three distinctive string sheets, use them together in a single composition. Before you begin, however, step back from your string sheets and hang them on your work wall or lay them on the floor. Stare at them. Evaluate them using the exercise outlined on page 20. Then consider these scenarios:

✕ What might happen if I cut all my string sheets into narrow strips?

✕ What if I sew those narrow strips into a Log Cabin setting or some other traditional set? What other ways can I sew narrow strips together?

✕ What might happen if I cut my string sheets into wide strips?

✕ What might happen if I cut one of my string sheets into large squares, one into small squares, and use the third as filler fabric to follow the Floating Squares score on page 24?

✕ What might happen if I leave my string sheets whole? How would I combine all three with as few cuts as possible?

You also have the option of using a single fabric with your string sheets, as filler fabric or to create negative space, and the option of using single strips for joining your string sheets.

After imagining a few scenarios, choose one to explore. Here's the best part: If you've succeeded in creating distinctive, lyrical, and rhythmic string sheets through setting limits at the outset, your composition will be interesting and engaging.

AS I COMPOSED my Strings quilt (page 32), I was surprised by how my everyday surroundings—the sparkling mirror-image cityscape on the bay of San Francisco and the concrete and graffiti of my East Oakland neighborhood—bubbled up out of my unconscious. I did not strive to achieve the cosmopolitan, tribal tone of this quilt; it just emerged.

MATERIALS: My habit is to use solids only, but I challenged myself to use prints with my solids. I pulled out my stash of vintage '70s fabrics. **(a)**

STRING SHEET LIMITS: I worked with only two variables to create rhythm in my string sheet sets: strip width and prints or solids. I didn't change colorways or value between sets. **(b)**

CUTTING STRING SHEETS: The natural lines of my ruler-free, hand-cut strips are slightly wavy.

SEWING STRING SHEETS: Of the two sheets shown, one is made of wide solid strips alternated with narrow print strips. The other has wide print strips alternated with narrow solid strips. I made five string sheets, ranging from 27" to 54" (69 cm to 137 cm) wide, each with a different sequence of wide/narrow and solid/print strips. The distinction between my sets was subtler than I expected, but it works. **(c)**

COMPOSITION: I decided to explore a chevron setting for my string sheets. **(d)** Because of my lack of control and familiarity with the chevron pattern, I had no clear method for cutting my sheets at angles in an efficient way. My "mistakes" added dynamically to the composition.

I paid a lot of attention to the space around my patchwork as I was working, and this played a major role in the final outcome. I used shades of gray to retain the negative space highlighting the edges of my string composition and to define a permeable border. Occasionally I used single strips of navy or yellow to break the center mass of the strings. **(e)**

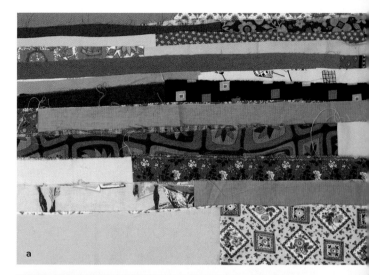

a

b

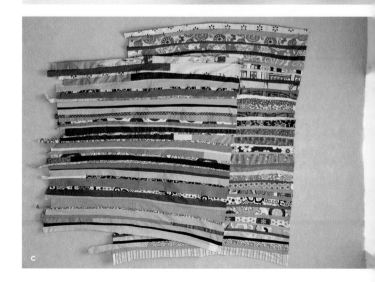

c

LINE

Lines separate space and define the edges of objects. They mark where a thing begins and ends in the space that surrounds us. Lines are conceptually indispensible in helping us define our world. The quality of a line is able to communicate emotion, direction, form, and texture.

The seam line is the structural essence of patchwork, ubiquitous yet taken for granted. We mostly imagine patchwork in terms of shape, but in reality, the seam line is the heavy lifter: defining, dividing, and holding together the space of our patchwork quilts.

If I were to make string sheets using a ruler to measure and cut my strips, the outcome would be generally less interesting and limited because the quality of the line would *always* be perfect, mechanical, impersonal, and one-dimensional. The Strings score is an opportunity to explore the lyrical qualities of a line as a design element.

When I look around at the lines in my loft, I notice the structural lines that make the building function. I see the crisscrossing diagonal lines of the beams that hold up the roof. I see the lines of large and small pipes running across the ceiling and of steps and shelving, and the outlines of a table and chair. All of a sudden I'm living in a patchwork quilt!

Shift the way you view your environment by paying more attention to the contour lines of things than to the shapes of things or the things themselves. What do you notice about the quality and arrangement of lines surrounding you?

Beth Lehman (far right) set simple limits for her string sheets, alternating a gray fabric with only one other fabric in each set that changes for a monotone effect. It's modern minimal.

Barb Mortell (near right, top) also used limited colors and values. She achieves an interesting checkerboard bargello-like effect by crosscutting her sheets into narrow- to medium-width strips.

Veronica Hofman-Ortega (near right, bottom) took the score in a completely different direction by creating complex string sheets made with many fabrics of similar hues. Her blended crosscuts are narrow and recombined to create a sparkling, woven tapestry of color.

Barb Mortell   Beth Lehman
Veronica
Hofman-Ortega

Improv Is . . . a "YES, AND" Conversation
·· improv round robin ··

YES, AND... is one of the guiding principles of improvisational theater. In order for a scene to unfold, the performers on the stage must affirm whatever their partner offers and then take it a step further. It's a process of listening to and accepting what is given and then responding and building on that offer. YES, AND is also a very effective way to join and build a satisfying conversation.

By saying YES, you are affirming what has been said. By saying AND, you are adding to the conversation in a related way. If one of these two elements is missing, the conversation stagnates and, as they say in improv theater, the scene falls flat.

If you say, "The snow outside today is beautiful," and I respond, "Yes it is." You may feel met, but the conversation ends. If I were to negate your original offer and say, "YES the snow is beautiful, BUT it's a real drag," you may feel judged, unheard, or shut down. You started a conversation about how inspired you felt by the snow, and I turned the tone of the conversation toward complaint.

If I respond, "YES it's beautiful, AND this is the perfect snow for a snowball fight," you might respond, "YES it's perfect for snowball fights AND for building a snow- man." Now there's something to talk about, and we've established a connection.

The YES, AND conversation is the improvisational model for the Improv Round Robin. Improvising is all about relationships and most often occurs in a community. The Improv Round Robin group workshop score is an opportunity to improvise with others through the medium of patchwork.

┌
│ **SCORE #3 SYNOPSIS**

   ✗ Introduce the YES, AND improvisational process.

   ✗ Establish rules and group procedures.

   ✗ Demonstrate techniques and prepare the mind.

   ✗ Sew in twenty-minute rounds.

   ✗ Evaluate the group process and wrap up.

Score for Improv Round Robin

This is a community-building score that can be done face to face with other quilters or organized as a long-distance exchange project. Each participant starts a quilt and passes it on to others to work one at a time. For this book, I hosted a round robin as part of Stitch Modern in Oakland, California.

step 1. introduce the YES, AND method of improvisation

Introduce the YES, AND conversation as a model for how to improvise several patchworks at once in a group. The goal of the Improv Round Robin is for each participant to accept and build onto each patchwork as it is passed around in a YES, AND way, through "listening" to the patchwork, noticing the patterns that are emerging, and then adding pieces onto it in a way that amplifies the conversation.

The beauty of the Improv Round Robin is that participants must work with the fabrics of others to explore and respond to patchwork patterns to which they don't habitually gravitate.

You will notice that some of the patchwork "conversations" you receive will be easier to enter than others, just as in spoken conversation. The goal is to be flexible and responsive to whatever the patchwork is saying and to add to it cohesively within the set time limit.

Beyond being connected to the conversation, there is no grand plan to adhere to. Conversations flow. There's no going back, and there are no mistakes. Be bold with your joins. Ramp up the volume, just as you would when you are enjoying a really great conversation with friends, by increasing the scale of your response, especially as the quilt tops increase in size.

step 2. specify the fabrics needed

Advise participants to bring the following fabrics:

GROUP OF CURATED FABRICS: These are the fabrics your quilt will be made from. I recommend approximately three yards (2.7 m) of large scraps and two or three ¼- to ½-yard (25-cm to 50-cm) selvage-to-selvage cuts. Having a cohesive set of curated fabrics, with a range of values and a focused group of colors, will make for a better outcome. I also recommend throwing in small amounts of a few rogue fabrics that clash or go counter to your aesthetic.

1 YARD (1 M) OF YOUR "SIGNATURE" FABRIC: You will add this fabric to every quilt you work on during the Improv Round Robin. I call it a signature fabric because it functions to "sign" the sections of patchwork you create. There is no way to choose a fabric that will "go" with everyone's quilt, so don't bother fretting over it!

CONTAINER: A bag, box, or basket for your curated fabrics, so they can be easily passed on between rounds.

step 3. establish rules and review procedures

The only patchwork technique that I strongly discourage is the technique of slashing through a composition and reordering it. Unless the precedent of slashing was set at the beginning, this can be disrespectful of the conversation, like rudely interrupting a person in mid-speech. The only other time it is acceptable to slash through the work of someone else is when a major construction flaw renders future additions technically impossible or extremely difficult. For example, when a section is added in such a way that an inset

seam would be required to build onto it, the misfit piece might need to be cut off due to time constraints.

step 4. demonstrate techniques

Before the rounds begin I demonstrate the techniques for Equalizing Patchwork Sections (page 122), Ruler-Free Patchwork (page 124), and Template-Free Layered Curve Patchwork (page 136). After the rounds are commence I stop the clock to demonstrate Darting (page 128) and Ruler-Free Patchwork with Large Sections (page 130) as the need for these techniques arises.

step 5. prepare the mind

Just before the participants begin, I introduce them to two exercises helpful in preparing the mind for spontaneous improvisation. First, address any anxieties people have about the process using the Mind Tool for Undoing Anxiety on page 55. Then ask everyone to return to his or her sewing machine for the Centering Exercise on page 47.

step 6. commence the rounds

Each round in the day-long workshop is twenty to thirty minutes long with an alert given five minutes before the end of the round to notify everyone that time is almost up. During the first half of the workshop, keep rounds at twenty minutes to encourage spontaneity.

FIRST ROUND

In the first round, work with your own set of curated fabrics to create a patchwork section that opens the conversation for your quilt. To help participants stay focused on what they want to "say," I ask people to work in silence during this first round only.

At the end of the time limit, stop where you are, put your opening patchwork section and its curated fabrics in your container, and prepare to pass it clockwise to your neighbor on the left and receive a container from your neighbor on the right. Keep your signature fabric at your sewing machine. The signature fabric does *not* get passed.

PASSING

With everyone present and passing at the same time, containers holding the patchwork sections and curated fabrics are passed forward clockwise once after the first round, twice after the second round (two people to the left), three times after the third round (three people to the left), and so on.

SUBSEQUENT ROUNDS

After the first round, advise the participants to respond to the conversation that was started in the patchwork section they receive. You add to the section using the fabrics in the container plus a piece of your signature fabric. You can use as little or as much of your signature fabric as you feel is appropriate to the goal of creating a related, cohesive patchwork composition and clarifying the conversation as much as possible.

In later rounds, as the patchwork gets larger, extend the time limit to thirty minutes per round. Encourage participants to amplify the conversation by working with larger shapes to scale up the patchwork, while continuing to clarify and build the YES, AND conversation.

step 7. evaluate the process

Finish the last round at least twenty minutes before the end of the workshop. Gather as a group in a circle, with each person holding up the quilt top made with their own set of curated fabrics so that everyone can see. Take a minute to appreciate the outcome.

Do the Evaluation Exercise on page 20 together. Take turns sharing surprises, discoveries, satisfactions, and dissatisfactions about the improvisational round robin process and the results. Practice connecting to and building on people's shares by saying YES, AND.

step 8. close the conversation

Once you get your round robin home, go ahead and continue the conversation, or bring it to a close by cleaning up trouble spots and adding sections to balance the conversation or borders to bring your quilt to a desired size.

THE EAST BAY MODERN QUILT GUILD HOSTED
a six-hour Improv Round Robin as part of Stitch Modern,
an annual month-long event of workshops, lectures, and an
exhibition organized to showcase modern quilting, which
they graciously allowed me to document. It was held at the
Piedmont Arts Center near Oakland, California.

FABRICS: My curated fabrics included a value and hue range
of solid purples and greens with a few yellow zingers. I chose
to use a solid white fabric as my signature piece.

ROUND 1: Here is how I started my conversation **(a)**, but I still
had time to say a little more before the first round ended. **(b)**

ADDITIONAL ROUNDS: I participated in the conversation
started by others. I'm pondering where to add my signature
fabric. **(c)**

EVALUATING: This is how the conversation of pattern unfolded
in my quilt. I'm quite pleased with the outcome! **(d)**

CLOSING THE CONVERSATION: When I got my round robin
home, I noticed some trouble spots where the quilt was warped.
It was easier to remove some of the misfit pieces than correct
them. I added borders to two sides to complete the conversation
and increase the finished size. I also rotated the quilt a quarter
turn clockwise to designate the top. You can see my finished
quilt on page 40.

CENTERING EXERCISE

I like to begin my studio work sessions by getting centered. When I am present to myself, I am more present to my process and experience more flow. You may have your own centering ritual. If not, here is a simple five-minute exercise to try.

Start by sitting in your chair and finding a posture that will support your centering.

Next bring your attention to the bottoms of your feet and plant them firmly on the floor. Rest your hands on your thighs.

Find a resting spot for the eyes or close them.

Bring your attention inward. Begin noticing your breathing.

Let your attention float to the bottoms of your feet.

Feel the connection between the bottoms of your feet and the floor.

Let your attention float up from the bottoms of your feet, through your shins, to your knees, and then from your knees to your sit bones.

Pause here, feel the weight of your body pressing down on the chair, notice the effects of gravity on your body and the support your chair provides.

Notice your spine rising up from between your sit bones . . . follow its natural curve upward . . . and at the top of your spine your head balances gently.

Let your shoulders drop down.

Soften your belly, and your diaphragm . . .

Notice breathing in and breathing out.

Notice how your spine lengthens, your chest expands; your shoulders drop as you breathe in.

Notice how your belly softens and your energy flows in and down as you breathe out.

Over the next several breaths, follow your in breath up, and follow your out breath down, to your center, the space behind your belly button in front of your spine.

Breathe in, breathe out and drop down into your center.

Pause here at your center long enough to connect with your most authentic self.

Make room within your center for all that you are feeling.

When you're ready . . . let your energy rise up through your core . . . bring your attention out through your eyes, by widening your peripheral vision, taking in the full context of your surrounding.

When you are ready . . . bring your attention through your eyes to the colors and fabrics in front of you . . . Begin to work silently.

Notice how centering has changed your experience of the present moment.

score #3

·· improv round robin ··

The East Bay Modern Quilters know how to listen and communicate! Each of these quilts was passed along and worked on by at least eight different people over the course of the one-day workshop. It's amazing to see how each quilt displays a distinctive and well-evolved conversation. One speaks about open space, another radiates shafts of color, another facets of a gem, others blocks, stripes, and wedges. The diversity and unity evident in the outcomes of this particular Improv Round Robin reflect a community of quilters who are respectful, supportive, and in sync with each other.

49

Improv Is . . . Letting Go of Expectation
·· patchwork doodle ··

Our ability to plan is a uniquely human characteristic. We all love to make plans. Usually when I catch my mind wandering, I find myself in the midst of making some elaborate plan for the future. I'm thinking through every detail, going over all possible contingencies, so that I will be able to execute my plan perfectly and everything will happen just as I envision it. With a plan in place, I feel in control. However, most of the time, my plan never quite plays out the way I expect it to, and even when it does, I'm often left feeling unsatisfied because the experience didn't nourish me in the way that I had hoped.

In life and in patchwork, it's difficult to let go of expectations and move forward without a clearly defined plan. Being on the edge of unknown territory can be both frightening and exhilarating. To work through it takes a little courage—to accept and affirm your decisions along the way—and a good dose of curiosity.

Trust your process of self-discovery. Stay flexible and responsive to whatever comes along. If your expectations start raining on your party, invite them in to have a seat on the sideline and watch you dance!

Score for Patchwork Doodle

The definition of doodling is to draw or scribble aimlessly or to play or improvise idly. Doodling is directionless in the sense that the doodle can end up going in any direction. However, it is not random. There is a natural responsive flow to doodling. Marks are made and then responded to with more marks until the page is full. The responsive process of doodling is the improvisational model for this score. This process is very similar to the YES, AND conversation explored in Score #3, but this time you are working alone and saying YES, AND to yourself and to the patchwork as it evolves.

This score provides an opportunity to construct patterns with simple shapes outside of a traditional block setting. Intersperse your shapes with negative space to further expand the repertoire of pattern possibilities.

step 1. experience doodling

Before beginning your Patchwork Doodle, take ten minutes to doodle with pencil or pen on a blank sheet of paper. What did you notice? How did your doodle unfold? Did you think ahead and try to draw an image in your mind, or did you just start making marks on the paper and then add to those marks? Did your doodle come out the way you expected? Did you enjoy the process? How do you like the outcome?

The purpose of doodling on paper is to experience the responsive *process* of doodling. The doodle you draw is *not* the plan for your patchwork.

Like the experience of doodling on paper, the goal of your patchwork doodle is to create a composition responsively, one step at a time, and to have fun. Resist the urge to plan your composition ahead of time. Practice letting go of expectations.

step 2. gather your fabrics

SCRAPS: Scraps are the perfect starting point for your Patchwork Doodle quilt because they provide a variety of randomly precut shapes to inspire your doodling, and they can be used freely without concern over "wasting" fabric.

NEGATIVE SPACE FABRIC (OPTIONAL): I recommend choosing a negative space fabric in contrast to your scraps. For instance, choose a neutral tone if most of your scraps are colorful. Choose a solid if your scraps are mostly prints. Use this fabric interspersed with your scraps to create negative space either throughout the quilt or along the outer rows or borders.

step 3. explore simple shapes

Use the techniques for Ruler-Free Patchwork (page 124), Ruler-Free Strip Piecing (page 127), and Template-Free Layered Curve Patchwork (page 136) to patch together simple shapes without the use of precision tools or templates. Begin by choosing one shape you want to explore and repeat it several times. You may choose to intersperse your negative space fabric between iterations. As you repeat your shape, you are free to let it evolve. Do not plan beyond creating this one row, which can be the length or width of the intended size of your quilt.

Here are a few simple shapes you might explore:
Squares: 1-patch, 4-patch, Square-in-a-Square
Triangles: half-square, quarter-square, equilateral, isosceles, scalene (wonky)
Strips: single strip, strings, cross, Rail Fence, Log Cabin, or Half Log Cabin
Other Shapes: rectangles, hexagons, curves, diamonds

step 4. construct the quilt one step at a time

Say YES to the row you just made AND build the next row by exploring a different simple shape in response to the first.

Construct your quilt row by row, with each new row responding to the previous row. Affirm, accept, and respond to each row as your quilt unfolds without any predetermined, overarching plan. Focus on one row at a time. Don't worry about what comes next.

A medallion construction is an alternative to building row by row. With this option, begin with a center section, and construct your patchwork doodle border by border from the center out.

With either a row-by-row construction or a center-out medallion construction you may want to employ the technique for Approximate Measuring (page 132). As your patchwork sections become larger than your rotary mat, follow the steps for Ruler-Free Patchwork with Large Sections on page 130.

step 5. develop the composition

Combine more than one simple shape in your rows or sections. For example, create a row with strips and squares, strips and triangles, or triangles and squares. Intersperse negative space with simple shapes in such a way that allows the space to connect and flow between rows. Play around and elaborate to develop unique patchwork combinations for each row.

A theme or direction will likely emerge as your composition grows. Let your patchwork be your guide and go with the flow.

Your quilt is finished when it reaches its target size or when you feel/think it is complete. Apply the Evaluation Exercise on page 20 to evaluate your process and outcome.

"When you use scraps,
you always get a surprise."

—Kate Brown, from
Accidentally on Purpose by Eli Leon

AS MY DOODLE QUILT (PAGE 50) EVOLVED, I was surprised that this piece, once again, reminded me of my surroundings—the docks and marinas of the Port of Oakland. I discovered that I could start with the intention of building a quilt from scraps using simple shapes, and I could end up manifesting anything—in this case the image of a marina fairyland!

DOODLE: As you can see, my doodle looks nothing like my finished quilt. It was just a warm-up. (a)

FABRICS: I chose to use solid scraps; my negative space fabrics were light gray and grayish purple with some blue plus mustard solids of similar value.

SIMPLE SHAPES: I made my first row from a section of four patches (b) that I combined, sliced, and sewed into a mass of rectangles joined to a section of Wonky Log Cabins. (c) I followed that with rows of strings, a Rail Fence variation, and curve shapes. (d)

a

c

d

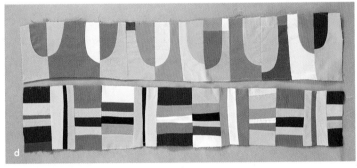

e

b

CONSTRUCTION: I switched from building row by row to adding borders on all four sides. In the outer borders, I began combining simple shapes with negative space and discovered some very interesting configurations, like this chevron triangle built with a Log Cabin construction. **(e)** The effect of mixing negative space with simple shapes opened up many new pattern combinations.

COMPOSITION: As I built more rows, flag-like shapes emerged into a nautical theme, and I went with the flow. I composed most of the quilt in one direction **(f)**, but toward the end I rotated the entire quilt a quarter turn clockwise to complete it as shown finished on page 50.

mind tool
UNDOING ANXIETY

Anxiety isn't actually an emotion. It is a defense mechanism of the mind that keeps us from feeling emotions. As human beings, it's our nature to feel fear in the face of the unknown. But we can accept that the situation is indeed unknown and get curious instead. With improvisation, a lot is unknown. If working without a plan is creating anxiety in you, follow these steps to shift to curiosity.

List the thoughts that are creating anxiety in you right now.

Notice your negative predictions. For instance: My quilt isn't going to look good; I'm not going to like it; I will be wasting my time and my materials; I'm going to make a mistake; I'm too much of a control freak and won't enjoy this process; I won't be able to succeed at the techniques; my quilt isn't going to lie flat if I don't use a ruler.

Ask yourself, "Can I predict the future?" Realize that your negative predictions of the future have no basis in reality. Even if you are 90 percent sure, based on past experience, that you won't be able to make pieces fit together without a ruler, there is no way you can know for certain you will be unable to succeed this time around. Each moment is new and full of possibility.

Take a moment to hold the experience of anxiety caused by making negative predictions in one hand and the experience of being curious about the unknown in the other. Which do you prefer?

Get curious and see what happens!

SCORE #4: Patchwork Doodle

IMPROV GALLERY

score #4

·· patchwork doodle ··

Lucie Summers's patchwork doodle
(far right) is all about curves. It is a fresh,
uncensored exploration of curves built in
sections from the inside out, from top to
bottom, left to right, layered and slashed,
and finally combined into a playful whole.

Sharon O'Brien's doodle (near right),
on the other hand, has a sweet nostalgic
feel. It seems to have begun with a
central panel, which was then flanked by
angled panels that asymmetrically
mirror each other and, finally, wrapped
with a permeable border.

Sharon O'Brien   Lucie Summers

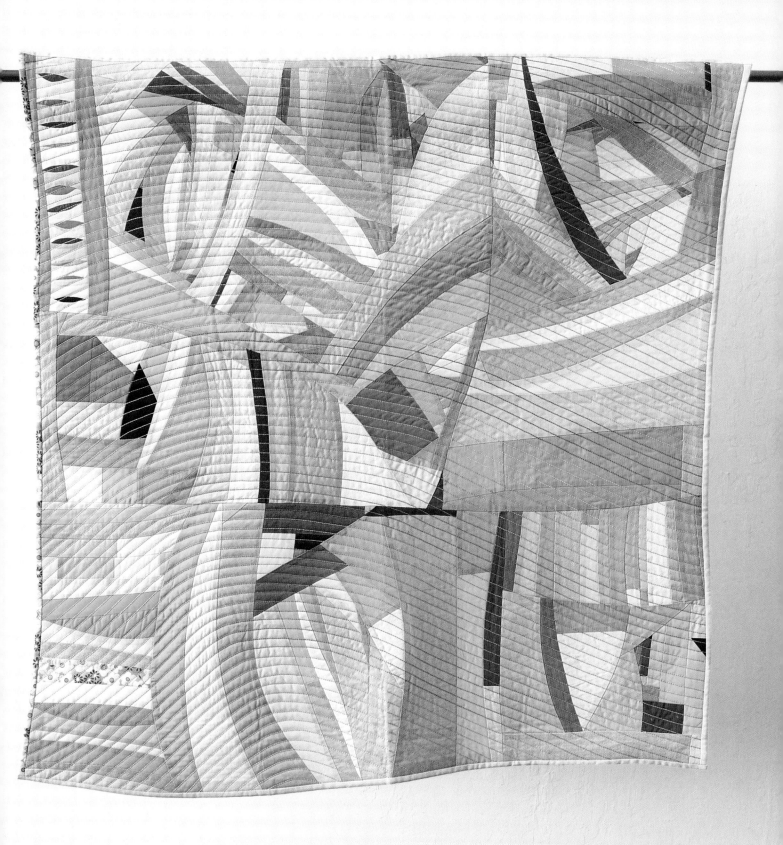

Improv Is . . . Figuring It Out
·· rhythmic grid ··

Sometimes life is a puzzle that requires a little creative figuring out. When faced with a challenge, it's an opportunity to "think outside the box." But exactly what does thinking outside the box require from us?

At the least, it requires a willingness to take risks and make mistakes. At the most, we have to be willing to face the prospect of failing. It's scary stuff.

On the other hand, figuring things out your own way can be fun. As a child, my younger brother's idea of a good time was taking apart his newest toy to see how it worked. He couldn't always put the toy together again, but it didn't matter because he was making his own discoveries.

When things aren't figured out for us, we have the freedom and permission to get it done any way we can. If there are no instructions for how it has to be done, then our natural ingenuity has a chance to shine.

✗ Choose fabrics and estimate amounts.

✗ Build a base row from units of sashed squares.

✗ Construct a rhythmic grid by building and adding one row at a time.

✗ Add borders by building outer rows with a different colorway of fabrics.

Score for Rhythmic Grid

This score is based on an African-American quilt in Eli Leon's collection made by Marzella Tatum. The subtle rhythmic shifts in the grid are accomplished with variations of the sashed square, also known as the Square-in-a-Square block pattern. Like my brother with his toys, I had to take this quilt apart and reconstruct it for myself to see how it worked.

The Rhythmic Grid is a patchwork puzzle to be figured out, like a Rubik's Cube but with an infinite number of solutions. Jump in and enjoy the confusion while working toward the goal of creating a rhythmic zigzagging grid using simple squares and sashing. Take comfort in knowing ahead of time that getting lost is part of the solution.

This score provides an opportunity to explore your sense of rhythm while introducing the improv patchwork technique of Approximate Measuring (page 132). As Marzella Tatum said about her process making this quilt in *No Two Alike* by Eli Leon, "I placed my pieces til I got them to go like I wanted them [and] just cut them to make them come out." It's as simple as that! The beauty of the quilt will come from the journey of problem solving, not from preplanning a solution.

"Take what you have and make what you want out of it."

—Roberta Johnson, from *Accidentally on Purpose* by Eli Leon

step 1. curate fabrics and estimate amounts

Estimate fabric amounts for the components listed below for the size of quilt you want to make, from mini to king. How big will your squares be? How thick will your sashing be? How many squares in each row? How many rows? It's okay to do a little math to figure out approximate amounts. My preference is to skip the math and throw pieces of fabric onto the design wall or floor and eyeball the amounts needed to reach my target size, plus extra for seams. If your estimates run short, substitute fabrics similar in value and color as needed. (See Making Do on page 67.)

Here are the basic pattern components of the Rhythmic Grid patchwork puzzle.

Fabric A: Center Squares   **Fabric X: Border Squares**

Fabric B: Center Sashing 1   **Fabric Y: Border Sashing 1**

Fabric C: Center Sashing 2   **Fabric Z: Border Sashing 2**

When choosing your fabrics, first consider how the value and color differences between the center squares fabric and the two different center sashings might affect the outcome of your pattern.

Next correlate color and/or value shifts between the center fabric A with the border fabric X, B with Y, and C with Z. Do you prefer a dramatic or a subtle shift between the center and the borders?

step 2. build a base row

First choose the width of your sashing. The width can be consistent or it can vary. Precut some sashing strips from both of your center sashing fabrics B and C.

Next consider the building blocks of the Rhythmic Grid puzzle. Your center squares (or rectangles) can be sashed with B and/or C on four, three, two, one, or zero side(s) as in Diagram 1 at right.

Diagram 2 shows the base row construction of my composition. Notice that it is a Courthouse Steps construction. Begin here *or* create an initial row from any combination of the sashed blocks shown on this page. However you choose to construct your base row will affect the solution to the puzzle.

Your base row need not be limited to four blocks; it can be many more depending on the scale you are working at and the desired size of your quilt.

1

2

step 3. create a rhythmic grid

Build at least three additional rows/columns on either side of your base row using center fabrics A, B, and C.

Shift the rhythm of each row, while maintaining the grid as much as possible, by using a combination of four-sided, three-sided, two-sided, and one-sided sashed squares/rectangles or a square/rectangle without any sashing at all, as pictured in Diagram 1. Use the improvisational technique of Approximate Measuring on page 132 to connect sashings B and C to form a continuous zigzagging grid from row to row.

At some point you may feel lost and unsure of what to do next, but go with the flow and allow accidents to happen. Resist the urge to plan or figure it out ahead of time. If a "mistake" interrupts your plan, it's probably your inner rhythmic wisdom intervening on your behalf.

step 4. add borders

Once the center is complete, create two opposing outer borders by shifting to correlating fabrics X, Y, and Z to continue the rhythm of squares and sashing.

step 5. evaluate your experience and results

Apply the Evaluation Exercise (page 20) after making your quilt top to assess what you've learned from the experience and to identify what you might do differently next time.

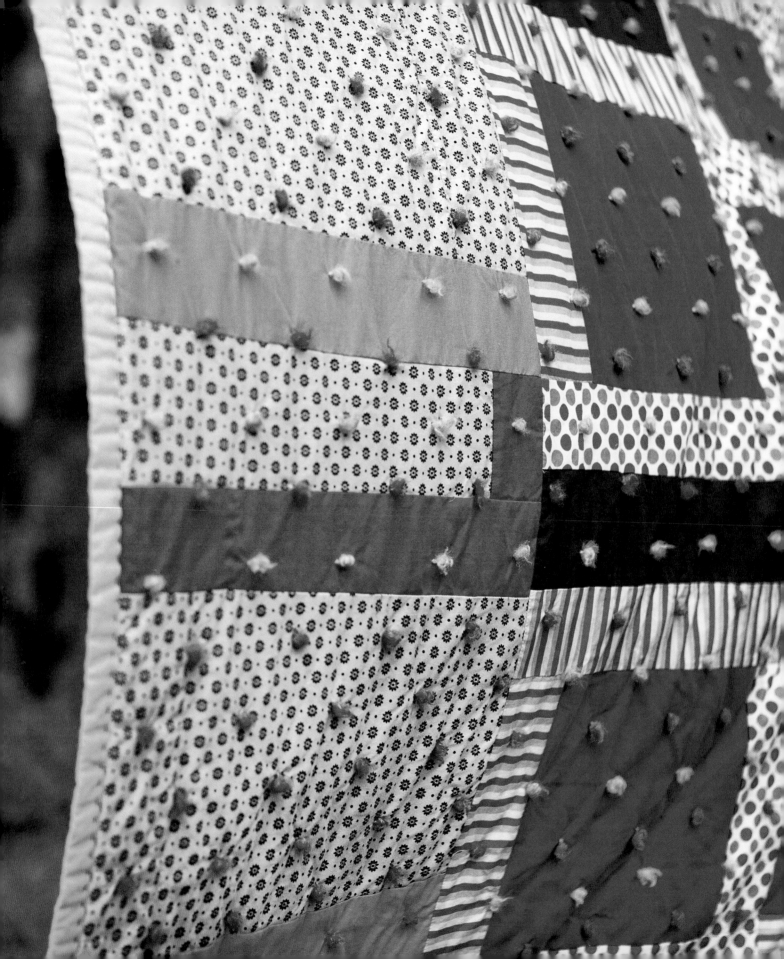

design consideration
THE MODERN PERMEABLE BORDER

Borders enclose, encircle, edge, bind, flank, and surround the center; they are the margin, edge, perimeter, and boundary. Borders were commonly seen as solid, unbroken lines that nothing can penetrate in either direction. This kind of solid boundary preserves identity, groups, and systems in stasis since no new influences can enter to disrupt, and potentially transform, the status quo.

Likewise a closed border on a quilt minimizes visual distractions and points the eye toward a single perspective of the pristinely pieced quilt. This impenetrable border crystallizes and supports an unchanging vision of perfection.

The broken-line borders introduced in African-American improvisational patchwork reflect a more inclusive, dynamic, and modern understanding of how borders and boundaries can function in quilts, in human development, and in our society. Broken-line, permeable borders—imagine the dashed line created by hand quilting—welcome difference, allow the exchange of ideas to flow and new influences to penetrate, and incubate change and transformation.

Boundaries are still important, however, so consider the ways you can create

permeable open borders that allow the eye to move and the patterns of your improvisational quilts to breathe and live. In my interpretations of the Patchwork Doodle Quilt (page 50) and the Strings Quilt (page 32), I created borders using negative space to permeate the visual edges of the central patchwork forms.

The Score for Rhythmic Grid (page 58) gives instructions for how to create a permeable border by shifting the colorway of the patchwork pattern in the border rows as it continues to penetrate to the edge of the quilt. In my interpretation of the Modern Block Improv Quilt (page 70) the permeable boundary is more subtly executed, but it's clearly there as a diagonal colorway and pattern shift in the bottom right corner.

Don't forget that bindings are thin visual borders as well. I sometimes do away with the visual intrusion of a binding by facing my quilts (page 165) or by using multiple fabrics that read as a broken line.

All of the contributor quilts reflect this shift away from closed borders. I encourage you to explore dashed line approaches to creating borders and sashings in your quilts.

"[Mother told me,] 'It ain't no harm in makin' no mistake. You might want to fix it a little bit different than I made mine.' And I fix it like I want it to satisfy me."

—Fannie Moore, from *Accidentally on Purpose* by Eli Leon

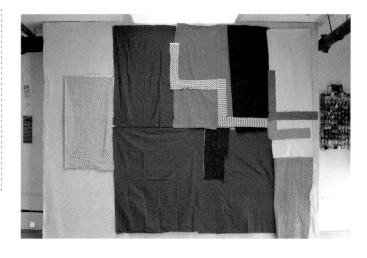

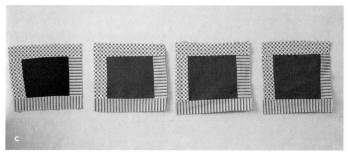

I ENJOYED DECONSTRUCTING and then replicating the classic African-American flexible pattern Square-in-a-Square to figure out how it ticked and write a score for it. Once my quilt (page 58) was completed, I was surprised by how different the rhythm was from end to end. I can visually "hear" the beat of this quilt.

FABRICS AND AMOUNTS: My quilt is 108" x 102" (274 cm x 259 cm). I threw fabric on my wall until it was covered. **(a)** I used shades of dark blue solids for the center squares A. I used a red/pink/yellow stripe for sashing B, and a red and pink dotted fabric for sashing C. I substituted a pale pink solid when I ran out of the red and pink dots. **(b)**

I transitioned the borders to three different prints for my squares X. I chose an orange solid for Y to correspond with B; I chose a red solid with some yellow added for Z to correspond with C. **(b)**

BASE ROW: I began my base row/column with four Square-in-a-Square blocks. **(c)** They are constructed like Courthouse Steps but are "disguised" because the matching sashing fabrics are adjacent to each other rather than opposite each other. I spaced apart the blocks with rectangles of my center square fabric A to make the base row. **(d)** It is the first center row on the left when looking at the finished quilt.

RHYTHMIC GRID: Once the first row was established, I continued the zigzags using the Approximate Measuring technique (page 132) to build three-sided blocks **(e)** and mixed up the beat by adding four- and three-sided blocks in the second row. I switched to mostly two-sided blocks in the third row **(f)**, except for one section sashed on one side, and one block sashed once at the top.

BORDERS: I transitioned the borders from navy solids to three different prints, the striped sashing B to an orange solid, and the red and pink dotted sashing C to a red solid. I intentionally substituted a bit of yellow sashing for red in one corner to add some unexpected zing. **(g)**

FINISHING: Once I made all my rows, it was easy to sew them together to complete the quilt.

This quilt was so huge I used the Hand-Tying technique (page 162) to join the layers of the quilt. Alternating knots of red and pink wool yarn nicely echoed the dotted sashing fabric.

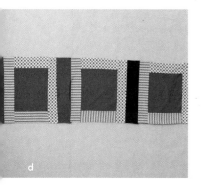

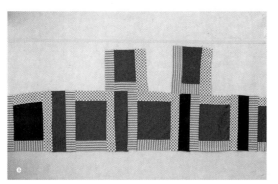

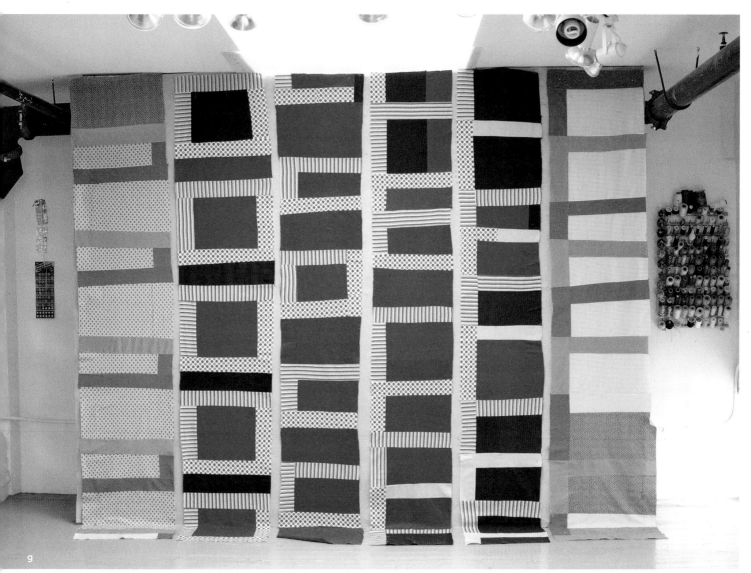

SCORE #5: Rhythmic Grid

MAKING DO

More often than not, contemporary quilt makers collect a lot of fabric. On the surface, this may seem like a design advantage, but in actuality, this abundance of choice can become overwhelming.

On the flip side, when you are forced to innovate with what you have and you do not have a lot, your improvisational skills are honed. One way to create the aesthetic opportunity to make do, even if your fabric stash is hefty, is to purposely limit your fabric amounts on the tight side at the outset of a project. If you are lucky enough to run out of a primary fabric, then you will be forced to make do with a substitution.

In the score for Floating Squares (page 24) I ask you to use all of the precut fabric, which forces you to innovate and make do.

Another method of making do, incorporating scraps in the forms they are found, requires tricky piecing strategies that can lead to unpredictable and surprising results.

Incorporating randomness into your process by pulling shapes blindly from a bag is yet another way of making do.

Making do with fabrics and patterning given to you by others, as happens in the Improv Round Robin on page 40, is another way to discover new territory in your patchwork.

Can you think of any more ways in which you can make do in your process?

RESTORE ATTENTION BY OBSERVING NATURE

Sometimes the results of improvisational patchwork are seen as random, but actually they are patterns of choice. The patterns of nature, on the other hand, are truly random and fascinating. They engage our attention effortlessly.

After a long stretch of focused decision-making in the studio, you may become unable to think clearly or act decisively. According to Attention Restoration Theory, you are probably experiencing directed attention fatigue, and it's time to take a break.

Your concentration will be refreshed after just fifteen minutes of watching the waves roll in, the clouds sail by, a pigeon in the park, or the shifting shadows of trees on a path; of listening to the sounds of birds; or of sensing the flow of wind through your hair. Observing the random patterns of nature will restore your rhythm of attention so you can return to your task with fresh eyes.

score #5

·· rhythmic grid ··

The first version of this score sent to the test quilters included an incorrect diagram for the starting row. Robin Cowie Green (far right) began her quilt before the diagram was corrected, thus rendering it impossible to create an unbroken grid. Robin's quilt reflects her bold journey of figuring it out and proves there is no right or wrong way to solve the puzzle.

Pamela Rocco (near right, top) adapted the score uniquely by varying the widths of her sashing, the size of her squares, and her relationships of color and value from row to row. It has a voluptuous quality of line and shape reminiscent of art deco.

Rossie Hutchinson (near right, bottom) chose to use multiple colors for her sashing and left off the borders. The distinctive, unequal rows of checkerboard sashing and the dark squares at the bottom left corner make her interpretation playful and light.

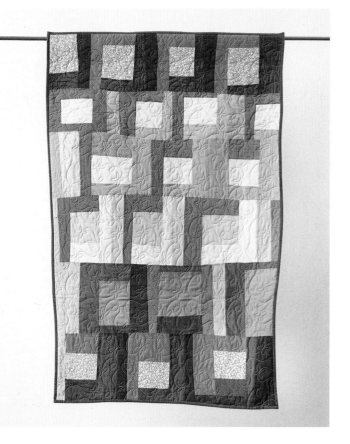

Pamela Rocco   Robin Cowie Green
Rossie Hutchinson

Improv Is . . . Flexible Patterning
·· modern block improv ··

I recently signed up for a beginner theater improv class, and the very first thing the teacher asked us to do was walk naturally. After we repeated our natural gait for a while, he asked us to change one thing about how we were walking. I began to swing my arms, another person nodded her head, and another snapped his fingers. This simple act of noticing a pattern, then making a change, is the basic building block of improvisational process.

> A quilt block pattern is generally understood to be unchangeable—a fixed entity to be repeated consistently within a single quilt. The only variations between blocks might be in color, fabric selection, or possibly value.

With a slight shift of mind, just about any traditional quilt block pattern can be conceived as a score for improvisational patchwork. The block pattern is repeated as a sequence of structural variations, and visual elaborations change with each repetition as you please. Conceived as a score, your block pattern becomes a framework within which you are free to explore, change, and even transform the structural boundaries of the block into something completely new. The block pattern becomes the limit, the container, the field of play, or the jumping off point for the improvisation.

> Flexible patterning requires and develops a flexible mind; it will display your creative process rather than your ability to reproduce a pattern consistently.

- ✖ Choose fabrics.

- ✖ Construct the initial block.

- ✖ Repeat the block, making structural variations.

- ✖ Find your flow.

- ✖ Elaborate on your variations.

- ✖ Combine blocks into a composition.

Score for Modern Block Improv / *FLYING GEESE*

Flexible patterning can be applied to any of your favorite quilt block patterns. If you have ever made a quilt with "wonky" Log Cabin blocks, you are already somewhat familiar with the method used in this score. However, there is a tendency for flexible patterning to become fixed in some popular block patterns. Avoid block patterns, like Log Cabin, that have been over improvised if you want to discover authentic new territory.

For this score, I chose to explore the Flying Geese block. It is a deceptively simple pattern that yielded much more variation than I expected.

This score introduces two improvisational techniques for composing with a variety of block shapes and sizes: Natural Shaping (page 134) and Patchwork Puzzle (page 134).

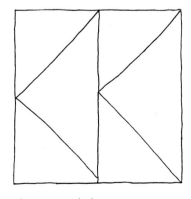

Flying Geese Block

"When I get it together, well I'm surprised at the quilt that I have made. It's so much different to what it's supposed to have been. It's a new pattern."

—Willa Etta Graham, from *Who'd A Thought It* by Eli Leon

step 1. curate fabrics

Begin with two fabrics of contrasting value in the amounts needed to reach the target size of your quilt. As the improvisation progresses, incorporate additional fabrics and colors as you please.

step 2. construct your initial block

Construct the Flying Geese block pattern as it is traditionally conceived out of the two contrasting fabrics but without using precision tools such as rulers and templates. Instead employ the technique for Ruler-Free Patchwork on page 124. If you are not familiar with how to construct this block, you will be glad to know there aren't any inset seams. You simply make two rectangles out of three right-angled triangles (one large and two small), then stitch the triangles together.

step 3. repeat the block and make variations

Repeat the block one or more times until you are comfortable with the construction and ready for a change. At your own pace, vary the structure of the block. Try all or some of these variations as a warm-up:

× Change the scale of the block—make it smaller and/or larger

× Change the proportions of the block—elongate it horizontally and/or vertically

× Change the proportions of the shapes within the block

× Simplify the block pattern

× Make the block more complex

× Alter and/or add additional colors or fabrics

× Shift the values of the block pieces

× Alter the orientation of the block setting

In what other ways can you vary the pattern?

step 4. discover your natural pace of change

Continue to put the block through a series of repetitions and variations. Let one variation lead to the next. Become familiar with each new variation, if need be, by repeating it to the point of boredom. Find your flow by cultivating an attitude of curiosity and exploration. Notice your inclinations to become entranced by certain variations and bored more quickly by others. Once you are in the flow, allow the pattern to evolve naturally. Incorporate additional fabrics and colors as you are moved to do so.

step 5. elaborate on your variations

Let variation build on variation. Choose a path that either delights you or scares you. Take the exploration as far as you can go. If one of your variations breaks through the limits of your initial block, feel free to ditch the previous variations and begin elaborating from there.

Don't be discouraged if you make a few duds. They are not mistakes; see them as necessary steppingstones to the next discovery. You do not have to use them in your final composition. As you create your blocks without precision tools, leave them in their natural shapes using the Natural Shaping technique on page 134 to clean them up.

step 6. combine units into a composition

Create enough blocks to make a quilt of your target size. Use Patchwork Puzzle (page 134), Ruler-Free Patchwork (page 124), and Equalizing Patchwork Sections (page 122) to combine all or most of the variations in a single composition.

step 7. evaluate your experience and results

Apply the Evaluation Exercise (page 20) after making your quilt top to assess what you've learned from the experience and to identify what you might want to do differently next time.

WITHOUT ANY PRECONCEIVED PLAN, I was delighted to watch my Modern Block Improv (page 70) evolve into a wonderful narrative of lions living deep in the jungle, imagining the faraway landscapes described in the stories of migrating geese.

FABRICS: I started with a dark brown and a light brown solid. With each new variation of the block pattern, I added a different bright solid in the blue to green range. On the last variation I went multicolored. During the composition construction, I added vintage prints to fill in gaps.

INITIAL BLOCK: I quickly discovered that there are multiple ways to create a simple Flying Geese unit. I got lost in the construction possibilities, which resulted in pretty good flow and lots of repetitions of the initial block. **(a)**

VARIATIONS: I began with simple things like changing the scale, changing the value, and adding an additional color. Then I began morphing the proportions of the units. Sometimes I used filler fabric to preserve my points. This added complexity to the blocks and became a natural variation. **(b)**

ELABORATION: After I had made a lot of units, I began playing around with the setting on my design wall. The possibilities seemed endless. This play was quite fun and generated several options for overall design patterns. I documented some of these variations with photographs in case I want to explore them in the future. **(c)**

a

b

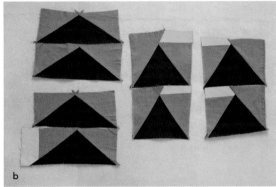

c

d

e

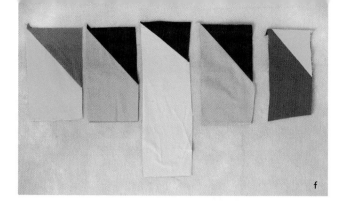

f

g

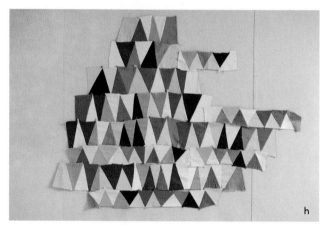

h

i

I was particularly excited about one setting variation that reminded me of an M. C. Escher–like box kite. I explored different elaborations on this setting including changing scale and switching values. I considered different settings for hinging them together. (d, e) I thought of making an entire quilt with just this variation but instead opted for including a large section of it in the composition.

COMPOSITION: I used the Patchwork Puzzle technique (page 134) to arrange and incorporate most of my blocks, but I still had some large gaps to fill.

I filled gaps across the top with simpler variations of the block. (f, g) I filled the gap on the left side with a groovy '70s lion print.

In the bottom right corner, I shifted pattern and tone dramatically by including smaller multicolored isosceles triangles pieced in continuous rows. (h) I used strips of printed fabric as needed to fill in gaps and equalize the section lengths before joining them to the rest of the composition. (i)

NATURAL SHAPING: I left my units in their natural shapes as much as possible. This flared out the sides of my quilt top, which I decided to preserve with minimal trimming. (See Natural Shaping of a Quilt Top on page 152.)

SCORE #6: Modern Block Improv

score #6

·· modern block improv ··

There were so many great quilts submitted in this category it was nearly impossible to narrow it down to three. Mina Kennison's interpretation (far right) is a modern classic with simple repetitions, subtly shifting colors, cut-off tips of triangles, and fearless use of negative space. This quilt has a flow that feels real.

Penny Gold's decision to work the score in the classic two-color combo of red and white (near right, bottom) integrates her major scale shifts and different angles into a whole that is greater and more abstract than its parts.

Susanna Heath (near right, top) ran her flying geese through their courses to create a sampler of ever-complex iterations in a modern interpretive set. She effectively flocked her repetitions in groupings that recall the curved space perspective of geese in flight.

Susanna Heath   Mina Kennison
Penny Gold

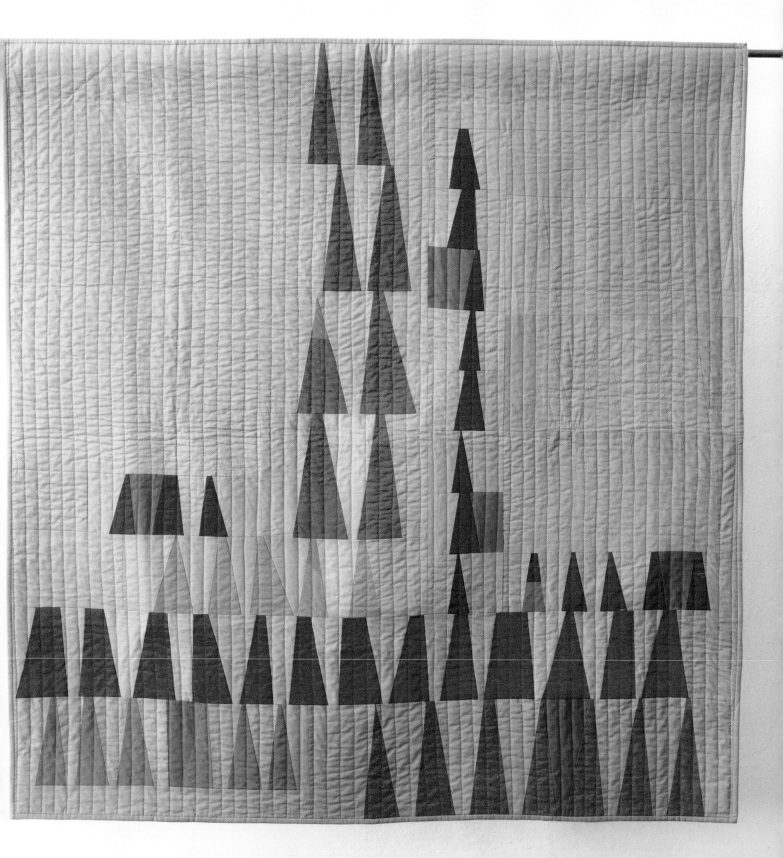

Improv Is . . . Experimenting and Getting Lost
·· layered curve ··

When was the last time you were actually lost? It's a rare experience with navigation devices and smartphones, which is good for me because I hate getting lost. But being lost isn't all bad. Have you ever become disoriented in a huge fabric shop or bookstore? You see some beautiful piece of fabric, or a book that leads you to the next, and soon you've even lost track of time. Or have you wandered around an unfamiliar foreign city while on vacation and come upon experiences that were never described in a guidebook? While getting lost may not always be comfortable, the experience is often interesting.

Being a good improviser requires practice and experience, and it takes a certain amount of enthusiastic experimentation and willingness to get lost to acquire that experience.

Cultivate the passionate, curious detachment of a scientist as you experiment with your patchwork. In the score that follows, there are options for experimenting with more or less control. If you get lost, imagine you're on holiday; eventually you are sure to find your way back, having discovered something new.

SCORE #7 SYNOPSIS

✗ Learn the simple technique for curve units.

✗ Choose fabrics.

✗ For each round: Consider options and cut base units.

✗ ROUND 1: Stack and cut one curve.

✗ ROUND 2: Stack and cut a second curve.

✗ ROUND 3: Stack and cut multiple curves.

✗ Combine units into a composition.

Score for Layered Curves

Exploring with any technique is a great gateway into improvisation. In this case your quilt or quilts will evolve out of a series of increasingly complex experiments you conduct to explore the limits and possibilities of Template-Free Layered Curve Patchwork (page 136). With each layer of complexity, the outcome will be less predictable. Enjoy getting lost.

"You'll start with one idea and that idea's not coming together like you want it to come, then you just say 'let's try it this way.' It won't come out in your first idea but it will come out into an idea that you like better than the first one."

—Laverne Brackens, from *Accidentally on Purpose* by Eli Leon

step 1. learn the technique

You can try Template-Free Layered Curve Patchwork (page 136) with scrap fabric or jump in and learn as you begin working the score.

step 2. curate your fabrics

Choose between three and nine fabrics of contrasting values for each of the three rounds: making single curve units, making double curve units, making multiple curve units. A distinct range of values will highlight your curve piecing. Change fabrics between rounds or use the same fabrics for each round. If you want to add fabrics along the way, that's okay too.

step 3. make single curve units—round 1

Cut at least three square or rectangular base units of equal size and stack them on top of each other, right sides facing up.

Cut a single curve through the stack. With right sides still facing up, mix and match the curve pieces. Flip and sew right sides together. Repeat until you have as many single curve units as you desire.

EXPERIMENT WITH LESS CONTROL

✖ Vary the size or shape of your base sections with each new stack.

✖ Vary the line of your cut with each new stack.

step 4. make double curve units—round 2

Create at least three single curve units as described above.

Restack the single curve units, orienting the curves in the same direction. Cut a second curve through the stack. Cut the second curve to echo the first curve, mirror the first curve, or cross the first curve without mirroring it. With right sides facing up, mix and match the curve pieces. Flip right sides together to sew. Repeat until you have as many double curve units as you desire.

EXPERIMENT WITH LESS CONTROL

✖ Apply any of the variations listed in Round 1.

✖ Mix single curve units of different sizes and lines in a stack. Add filler fabric if necessary to bring all units to the same size.

✖ Orient the direction of each curve differently within a stack.

step 5. make multiple curve units—round 3

Create at least three double curve units as described in Step 4.

Restack, cut, and sew as many times as you like to create multiple curve units.

Repeat until you have as many multiple curve units as you desire.

EXPERIMENT WITH LESS CONTROL

✖ Apply any of the variations listed in Rounds 1 and 2.

✖ Mix multiple curve, double curve, single curve, and base units in a single stack.

step 6. combine units into a composition

Before beginning your composition, pause and reflect on your experiments. What did you discover through trial and error? Did you play it safe? How much were you able to control the outcome? How much did you want to control the outcome? Did you take any risks? How did it feel being lost? Do the Evaluation Exercise on page 20.

As you consider your composition, know that you don't have to use all of the units. You can mix units from each round into a single quilt composition, or you may choose to keep the units separated by round and make a series of compositions. You can choose the most successful units from your experiments and duplicate the results to create more for your composition, while discarding the less successful units. You can set the units in a grid or you can offset them. You can cut them into smaller sections. You can offset them with irregular sashing. Refer to the Patchwork Puzzle technique (page 134) and the Design Consideration: The Modern Permeable Border (page 63) for additional guidance with composition.

EXPERIMENTING WITH Layered Curves taught me that order can quickly turn to chaos! The next time I employ the method of stacking and cutting curves, I will fine-tune my process to see if can discover more middle ground. (You can see my finished experiments on page 78.)

FABRICS: I worked with two color schemes: cyan, yellow, magenta, and black and red, green, blue, and white. I carefully chose a range of values and even took black-and-white images to test the range (see page 116 for more on color value). I also threw in an occasional orange base unit. **(a)**

BASE UNITS: I used a 14" (36 cm) square base unit for each round of experiments.

SINGLE CURVE UNITS: I cut approximately the same curve through each stack of units. I did not apply any of the complex options in the first round of experiments and maintained a lot of control. **(b, c)**

DOUBLE CURVE UNITS: I used the same color range and the same size base unit as above and made additional single curve units. I cut second curves that consistently mirrored the single curves. I maintained a lot of control over this second experiment as well. **(d)**

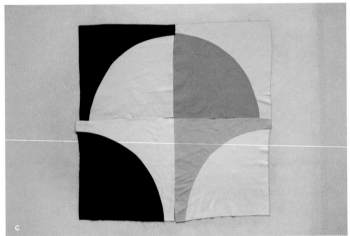

MULTIPLE CURVE UNITS: In this experiment, I loosened control of the outcome dramatically. I made additional single curve and double curve units in the same manner as before. In later stacks I mixed these in different orientations along with base units that had no cuts. **(e)**

COMPOSITION: I made twenty-five single curve units. Even in a grid setting there were many orientation options for the curves. **(f)** I made sixteen double curve units and again there were many orientation options. **(g)** I made nine multiple curve units, and the results were so chaotic that no matter how I set them, there was no order to be found. **(h)**

f

g

e

h

SCORE #7: Layered Curve

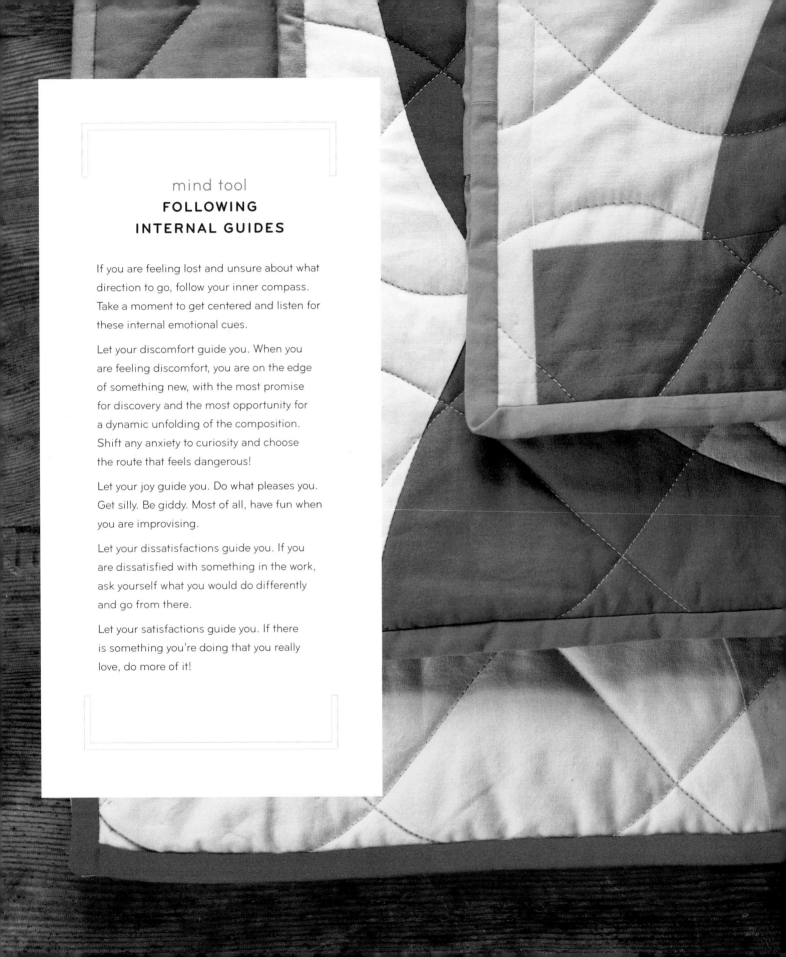

mind tool
FOLLOWING
INTERNAL GUIDES

If you are feeling lost and unsure about what direction to go, follow your inner compass. Take a moment to get centered and listen for these internal emotional cues.

Let your discomfort guide you. When you are feeling discomfort, you are on the edge of something new, with the most promise for discovery and the most opportunity for a dynamic unfolding of the composition. Shift any anxiety to curiosity and choose the route that feels dangerous!

Let your joy guide you. Do what pleases you. Get silly. Be giddy. Most of all, have fun when you are improvising.

Let your dissatisfactions guide you. If you are dissatisfied with something in the work, ask yourself what you would do differently and go from there.

Let your satisfactions guide you. If there is something you're doing that you really love, do more of it!

score #7

·· layered curve ··

Amy Friend successfully navigated the territory of a controlled experiment in her interpretation of the Score for Layered Curves. She created a composition that is both unified and chaotic. Her simple color palette helps to bleed and blend sections so that the underlying grid is less prominent. More importantly, she establishes a control shape—a distinctive yolk-like shape that appears in the corner of each section—that counterbalances the randomness of the rest of her curves. Her curved lines are marvelously fluid.

Amy Friend

Improv Is . . . Seeing With Fresh Eyes
·· bias strip petals ··

While reading through the book *The Quilts of Gee's Bend*, I was struck by how many of the Gee's Bend quilters learned to piece as young girls, typically around the age of eleven. It doesn't surprise me to think that learning to patch together scraps at such a young age would lead to imaginative, authentic compositions later in life. If you have ever made a quilt with the help of a child, it's likely she or he brought a fresh perspective to the process.

> Over my years of teaching, I've often noticed that some students with little or no prior experience making quilts pick up improvisation easier than some students who have years of precision patchwork under their belts. These newcomers have the advantage of seeing all the possibilities unhindered by the "rules" of quilt making. The Zen Buddhist Shunryu Suzuki spoke the truth when he said, "In the beginner's mind there are many possibilities, in the expert's mind there are few."

I've seen my own work evolve over the last twenty-five years. My earliest quilts are some of my best, even though I hardly knew what I was doing. They clearly display the enthusiasm and discovery of a beginner's mind. As I became more skilled and familiar with my techniques, materials, and process, my quilts often became static and self-conscious. Once I figure things out, I'm tempted to strive for perfection! Continuously challenging myself with tricky piecing situations is one way I've found to cultivate the fresh perspective of a beginner's mind in my work.

Score for Bias Strip Petals

This score introduces the advanced technique of Bias Strip Piecing on the Curve (page 140) along with an entire suite of supporting techniques: Ruler-Free Continuous Bias Strips (page 138), Darting Along the Curve (page 142), Darting Across the Curve (page 144), and Trimming the Curve (page 145). Take this opportunity to explore with the fresh eyes of a beginner as you are challenged to master these new techniques.

a

b

step 1. understand bias grain

Fabric grain affects the way the fabric will behave under the needle. There are three fabric grains:

✗ The lengthwise grain runs parallel to the selvage edge and the warp threads of the weave; it has the least amount of stretch.

✗ The crosswise grain runs parallel to the weft threads of the weave and is perpendicular to the selvage edge. It has a slight amount of stretch.

✗ The bias grain runs diagonally, at a 45° angle, to the crosswise and lengthwise grain of the fabric; it has quite a bit of stretch. **(a)**

The lengthwise and crosswise grains follow the actual warp and weft threads of the woven fabric, but the bias grain runs across the warp and weft. The bias does not follow a thread but cuts through the spaces between the warp and weft threads.

step 2. prepare your fabrics

Choose any fabrics you fancy. You will be cutting both the petal shapes and the bias strips from squares of fabric 18" (46 cm) and larger. For the smallest squares, you can select fat quarters, which are the fabric pieces measuring 18" by 22" (46 cm by 55 cm) sold in fabric stores (see Step 3). Choose a range of contrasting values for your bias strips so that all your effort to piece narrow strips on the curve will be visible. For the bias strips, you will need ½ to 1¼ yard (50 cm to 1.2 m) lengths of fabric (see Step 4).

step 3. cut petal shapes on the bias

I chose the petal shape to introduce the Bias Strip Piecing on the Curve technique (page 140) because of the score's curve trajectory. This technique can be applied to deeper clamshell curves or shallower scallop curves. Either way, the technique is best applied to large curves. Small curves can easily be built out using the Template-Free Layered Curve Patchwork technique (page 136).

Cut three or more petal or orange peel shapes, point to point on the diagonal, from squares ranging in size from 18" to 22" (46 cm to 56 cm) or larger. **(b)** Fat quarters work wonderfully for the 18" (46 cm) squares.

step 4. cut continuous bias strips

Create a stash of bias strips in a range of contrasting values using the Ruler-Free Continue Bias Strips technique on page 138. The bias strip width can range from 1½" to 4" (4 cm to 10 cm) wide, and you will want at least 18" (46 cm) squares to cut your bias strips from. I typically start with 22" to 44" (56 cm to 112 cm) squares.

step 5. ring petals with bias strips

Add bias strips along the concave curve of the petal shapes one strip at a time, using the technique for Bias Strip Piecing on the Curve, on page 140.

This is a challenging technique to master. The point here is to stretch beyond your comfort zone. You will encounter tricky piecing situations, and even make mistakes, that will force you to innovate. Start by adding at least two or three rings of bias strips around your petals to develop a feel for it. Continue to add as many rings as you desire.

Ringing your petals with bias strips is similar to building a Log Cabin block, except it's on the curve. So experiment with all the variations you might use when constructing a Log Cabin, such as varying the width or the value of your strips from side to side.

step 6. troubleshooting

Stretching too much and not stretching enough will cause bubbles or waves in the patchwork. Try to correct a distortion as soon as you notice it because it will only get worse and be harder to fix later. First, identify if the distortion is caused by overstretching or under-stretching the base curve.

OVERSTRETCHING: If your edge is wavy, then the base petal was overstretched while adding the bias strip. Correct this by removing the strip—simply undo the seam with a seam ripper. Steam-press both the base petal and the bias strip back to their original shapes and re-sew, remembering not to stretch the base curve quite as much.

Another option is to use the technique for Darting Across the Curve on page 144.

UNDER-STRETCHING: If there is an internal bubble along the curve or the freshly added bias strip curls up along the curve, then the base petal was under-stretched. Correct either of these situations using the techniques for Darting Along the Curve (page 142) and Trimming the Curve (page 145).

Feel free to use any sewing skills in your arsenal to master this technique.

step 7. choose a composition method

Once you've ringed a few petals, choose one of these three methods for setting your units.

BLOCK METHOD: Build your ringed petals into blocks. As rings are added and the corners of the block begin to fill in, sew only the length of strip needed to fill to the estimated edge of the block. Square up the block by trimming off any excess. **(c, d)**

Arrange four or more bias-strip petal blocks in a classic Orange Peel setting. **(e)**

APPLIQUÉ METHOD: Keep ringing your petals all the way around; when you have as many rings as you want on each petal, arrange them on a background and/or overlap them and hand appliqué them in place. See Hand Appliquéing for Large Shapes on page 150.

ARRANGE AND BUILD METHOD: Fully ring petals as much or as little as you like and arrange in any manner on your work surface. The ringed petals can be arranged whole or cut in segments.

Fill in the space between and around the petals one bias strip at a time until you reach the target size of your quilt. As the bias strips from different petals converge, add and sew the rings just past the projected intersection. Fold under one of the converging edges and appliqué in place. **(f)**

step 8. evaluate your experience and results

Apply the Evaluation Exercise, on page 20, after making your quilt top to assess what you've learned from the experience and to identify what you'd do differently next time.

e *Orange Peel Setting*

THE BIAS STRIP PETALS QUILT (page 86) was the most difficult quilt to piece in the entire book. It required a tremendous amount of patience and troubleshooting. Halfway through I decided something was needed to wake up the pastels. I added a psychedelic daisy print from the '70s and that did the trick.

FABRIC PREPARATION: I chose neutral shades of white and beige for my petals and cut my bias strips from solid pastels, a bit of black, and a few prints that reminded me of vintage sheets. My largest petals are 36" (91 cm) point to point. **(a)**

COMPOSITION: After sewing a few rings and trying a couple of different orientations, I decided on a daisy-like arrange-ment and started the process of joining them. I added more strips to some of the petals and moved my composition to the floor. **(b)** I did some tricky piecing to appliqué the centers together. **(c)**

After completing a section on the floor, I put the quilt back on the wall to evaluate and decide next steps, then it was back to the floor again. I continued in this way to add strips, slowly filling the space out to the projected edges and corners of the quilt. **(d)**

The quilt went back on the wall before the final shaping. Notice how the rings in the top right corner flare out past the straight edges of the quilt. **(e)** I debated for a long time whether to leave the top in its natural shape or trim it square. Ultimately, I chose to square it off.

SCORE #8: Bias Strip Petals

mind tool
CULTIVATING
BEGINNER'S MIND

It is not much of a stretch to see how beginner's mind—the practice of having an attitude of openness, eagerness, and lack of preconceptions when studying a subject—dovetails with the improvisational process. Here are just a few tips to cultivate seeing with the mind of a beginner.

Focus on questions, not on answers.

Respond to everything that comes with an attitude of not knowing.

Be willing and curious.

Do the exercises simply to see what your experience is.

Take one step at a time without worrying about the destination.

Keep an open mind about how to apply your experience and native wisdom in each new circumstance.

Let go of being an expert.

Celebrate mistakes.

Let go of self-consciousness.

Develop a sense of awe, a feeling of excitement and wonder.

Remember that we are mysterious, even to ourselves, so there is always the potential to see with fresh eyes.

mind tool
CELEBRATING MISTAKES

When you begin to figure things out your own way, follow your own patterns, and explore new territory, you are required to take risks and are bound to make mistakes.

Embarrassment was my habitual response to making a mistake before I signed up for an eight-week improv theater workshop as research for writing this book. Our teacher made us play impossible games at which we were sure to fail. He encouraged us to take risks, and whenever we made a mistake, he required us to throw our arms up and enthusiastically shout, "Whoopee!"

The teacher asked us to practice this at home for an entire week whenever we made a mistake. It was liberating.

Try celebrating your mistakes on your own or with a friend and compare notes afterward. It will change your life. If you burn the toast, throw your arms up and shout, "Whoopee!" If you sew a seam in backward—"Whoopee!" Practicing this for a week will shake you loose from embarrassment about imperfection. You will take more risks. You will live and create more spontaneously . . . and if you're happy and you know it, your patchwork will show it! Whoopee!

score #8

·· bias strip petals ··

Marion Shimoda (far right) adapted the score for Bias Strip Petals by using only part of her petal shapes by squaring them off and setting them in a grid with slivers of filler fabric. It's bold, direct, and abstract. Her interpretation seems to zoom into the seed or stamen at the center of the petals.

Latifah Saafir's interpretation (near right), in contrast, presents the plant in its environment. She used the bias strip curve piecing technique to good effect by choosing a single color to outline the petal shapes and then set the entire composition by appliquéing it to a two-tone background. It's clean, crisp, and feels symbolic.

Latifah Saafir   Marion Shimoda

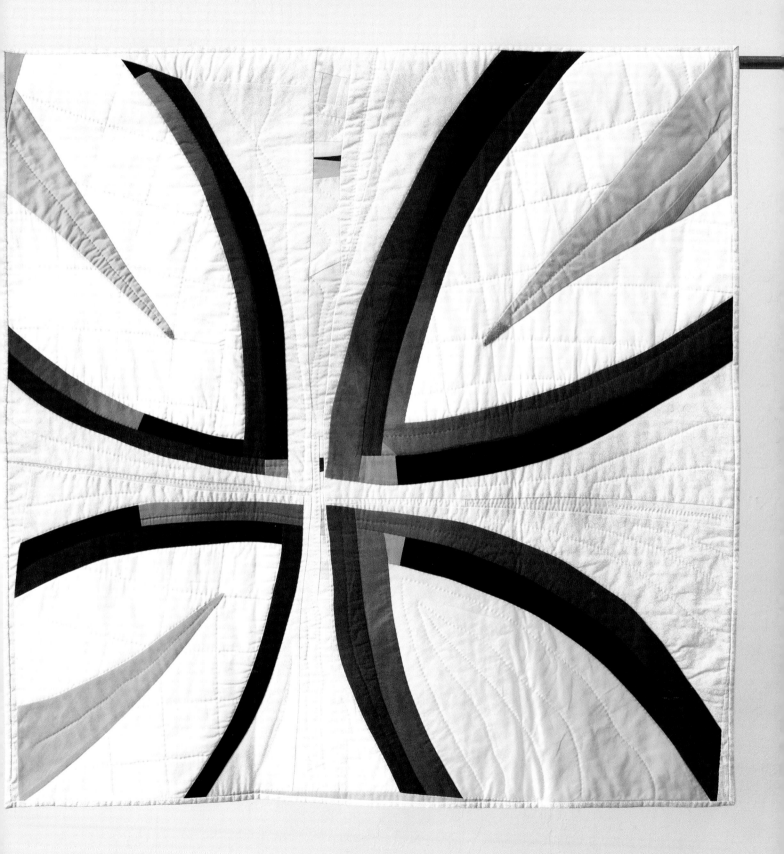

Improv Is . . .
Commitment on the Edge of the Unknown
·· get your curve on ··

Mastering advanced curve patchwork techniques can be challenging, but the bigger challenge is improvising a curvy composition.

It's easy to fudge and bypass a true experience of improvisation with Wonky Log Cabins or other patchwork forms of simpler construction, but template-free curve patchwork will require you to work on the edge of the unknown. There is absolutely no way to set a curve design in stone before piecing it together.

With curve patchwork, as soon as you sew it, you've changed it and the way it's going to fit with the rest of your plan. The only way to succeed is to take one step at a time without expectation. With each commitment and each element sewn into place, the landscape shifts. It's imperative to observe and meet each new situation with flexibility as it unfolds. This is the way trusting and enduring relationships between people unfold as well. It's as hard to do in quilting as it is in life!

When I teach workshops on curve improv, I watch almost every student hit a wall when faced with the composition. They move pieces around, settle on an arrangement, then move them around again. They are afraid to commit. As soon as they take the plunge and sew something together, they realize the composition they were so determined to execute has shifted. It's a stumbling block. However, something eventually clicks in the midst of their struggles, and I watch the patchwork begin to flow.

Hitting a wall, getting lost, and wrestling with commitment one step at a time is part of the process. I assure you the struggle is worth it, as your authentic voice starts to emerge in your patchwork. It will get easier as the lessons of improvisation sink in with practice.

Score for Get Your Curve On

I first introduced this score for creating a quilt with large curved sections made from wedged strips on daintytime.net as the Mod Mood Quilt. From its popular reception and from the amazing one-of-a-kind quilts it inspired, I realized that quilt makers are eager for flexible tutorials that nurture improvisational process and a multitude of variations. This is the one that started it all.

Even though curve patchwork is more challenging than straight-edge patchwork, it follows some of the same construction principles. This score introduces the techniques Wedge Strip Piecing on the Curve (page 146), Equalizing and Joining Curve Sections (page 148), and Hand Appliquéing for Large Shapes (page 150).

step 1. curate fabrics

Just as in the Score for Strings, page 32, curate at least three different fabric sets from which to cut wedge-shaped strips. Both large scraps and selvage-to-selvage yardage can be used in whatever combination of prints and/or solids, colors, values, volume, and contrast needed to create two or three distinctive curve sections.

step 2. define limits for wedge strips

Wedged curves are made with wedge-shaped strips of equal length that are wide on one end and narrower on the other. The parameters set for cutting strips of wedges will affect the breadth and shape of your curve sections. In the score for Strings, the only cutting variable is width. In this score, the

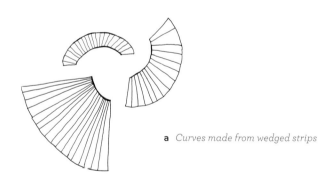

a *Curves made from wedged strips*

length as well as the width range of your wedge-shaped strips are limits to be considered and defined.

LENGTH OF WEDGE: Determines the volume of your curve sections.

WIDTH RANGE BETWEEN THE BOTTOM AND TOP OF THE WEDGE: Determines the arc length of your curve sections.

Set different limits for the length and width range for each set of wedges to piece a variety of wedged curve sections. Just start somewhere, and for the next curve apply a different set of limits to the wedges. There is no need to calculate ratios ahead of time to control outcomes. (a)

Your approach to setting parameters for your wedges can be intuitive, but if you really want to get mathematical about it, adapt the scale exercise outlined in Exploring Scale on page 28.

step 3. compose and set curve sections

Once you have several wedged curves created, throw them on your design wall or a horizontal surface to explore possible compositions and settings. Here are a few things to keep in mind:

✗ As you sew your curve sections together, the composition will change. Be flexible and constantly adapt your plan.

✗ Curves can be overlapped and shaped as they are cut to fit. Each time you do this, you create another wonderfully shaped curve scrap that can be incorporated into your composition. See Shaping and Incorporating Curves and Space on page 100.

✗ Break up curves with negative space. Often the space created by the placement of your curves can be more interesting than the curves themselves.

✗ Add single bias strips along the edges of your wedged curves (see page 140) to define them and add interest to the composition.

✗ Pay attention to bleeds and natural fits as you piece your curve sections. Refer to Patchwork Puzzle (page 134).

✗ If improvising with wedged curves to create a composition is too daunting, narrow your compositional limits and set your wedged curves into an abstract or traditional block setting like Grandmother's Fan.

As you compose with curves, you'll encounter plenty of tricky piecing situations. The Equalizing and Joining Curve Sections technique on page 148, along with techniques introduced earlier in the book, will get you through many of those situations.

With extreme curves or inset seams, I find it easier to piece by hand rather than by machine; the technique for Hand Appliquéing for Large Shapes on page 150 will show you how.

step 4. fill in background

Set a target shape and size for your finished composition. As you are joining larger and larger curved sections, build out to your target. Here are some tips and suggestions for filling in edges and corners:

✗ Use a filler fabric or a curated group of filler fabrics to enclose your circular composition.

✗ Build curve sections past the target size and shape then trim down.

✗ Use the Bias Strip Piecing on the Curve technique (page 140) to add rings around your curve sections all the way to the edges and corners, then trim to shape.

✗ Create a patchwork of strips, squares, crosses, or triangles to use as a foundation fabric and appliqué your composition in place.

✗ Bind the natural circular edges of the quilt and skip filling in the background all together.

✗ Apply these methods to create smaller straightedge sections containing one or two wedged curves. Arrange and sew into a composition using the technique for Natural Shaping of a Quilt Top (page 152) and Patchwork Puzzle (page 134).

step 5. evaluate your experience and results

Apply the Evaluation Exercise on page 20, after making your quilt top to assess what you've learned from the experience and to identify your next steps.

design consideration
SHAPING AND INCORPORATING CURVES AND SPACE

The composition possibilities for curve sections seem to be endless. This score creates its own making-do scraps each time you commit and join a new section. The key is to remember that wedge-strip pieced curve sections can be treated as foundation materials (page 34) and do not need to be used whole. They can be layered as much or as little as you wish. You have the freedom to shape the curve as you cut.

Each time you layer and cut, as in Steps 5 and 6 of Equalizing and Joining Curve Sections on page 148, there will be an interesting curve remainder you can work into your composition elsewhere. Because the remainder curve is hidden as you cut, the angles of the wedges in relationship to the curve will surprise you. When you incorporate these remainder curves into your composition, you will also be incorporating surprising negative space.

Test the limits to see how far you can push this process of layering, shaping, and incorporating the remainder curve sections in a single composition. What happens when you apply this process to straight-cut sections and other types of patchwork or scores in this book?

OCEAN WAVES WERE THE INSPIRATION for the blue-green wedges of my Get Your Curve On quilt (page 96). So it isn't surprising that my composition evolved into a spiral-eyed, DNA-oceanic, deep-sea, nautical abstraction, but it still wasn't what I expected!

FABRICS: I began with solid fabrics in mostly blue-greens and whites in light and dark colorways for my wedges.

WEDGE PARAMETERS: I created some very large curve sections with long narrow strips, 20" (51 cm) long and 1" to 3" (2.5 cm to 7.5 cm) wide; I also created some curve sections with shorter but wider strips, 9" (23 cm) long and 2" to 4" (5 cm to 10 cm) wide. I made a lot of curve sections that I didn't end up using but will save for future projects. **(a)**

COMPOSITION: I went through a variety of arrangements before I began to commit. **(b)** As I made decisions, the composition morphed and evolved.

BACKGROUND: As more of the composition came together, I began auditioning negative space fabrics. I wanted to soften and balance the intense colors of the wedge curves, so I chose a variety of pastels including yellow-beige, pale peaches and pinks, and the palest of lavenders. **(c)**

I eventually moved the composition to the floor. I used painter's tape to mark the target size of my quilt. I began to add the pastel filler fabric to equalize the lengths of my curve sections before joining them either with hand appliqué or by machine. **(d)** I continued to work in the round from the center out, adding filler fabric, single-bias strips, and more wedges to build the quilt to size.

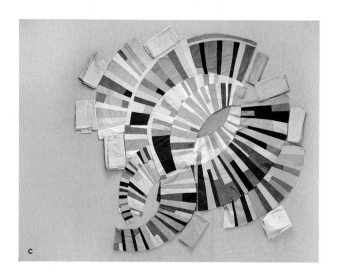

score #9

·· get your curve on ··

Carolyn Wong's traditional and kitschy fabrics blend to create a warm fruity universe of swirls for this score (far right). I like how she incorporates narrow, yet large, arching wedge-pieced curve strips around the dense nuclei of thicker wedges, forming tight curves. Her unconventional edge is a terrific example of natural shaping.

Drew Steinbrecher (near right) also discovers new territory in this score by setting his curves to face outward. The deliberate shaping of his wedges in a slightly awkward way adds to the quilt's unexpected modern charm. Also of note is his use of a pieced low-volume, neutral background and broken borders.

Drew Steinbrecher   Carolyn Wong

Improv Is . . . Telling a Story
·· showing up ··

Stories are filled with colorful characters, interesting locations, and conflicts and resolution. Storytelling, like quilt making, is all about creating meaningful relationships or narratives among disparate elements.

If you are a reader like me, you have multiple books in rotation on your bedside table. Occasionally, I read a book straight through, but typically I read one book for a while then switch to another. I may get back to books in my stack the next day, the next week, a month later, or sometimes never.

I usually put a book down because I've stopped resonating with the text. When I pick up the book again, I pay attention to what has occurred since I last read it for a glimpse at the shifting horizon of my unconsciousness. The book "shows up" for me in a new way.

The narratives of contemporary life are juxtaposed, like a pile of books on a bedside table. We know ourselves as much through the connections we make among different experiences, or through the rhythm of our attention, as we do from any single experience.

Eli Leon noted the attribute of juxtaposition—the side-by-side display of evolving, contrasting, or otherwise dissimilar elements—as a common thread in his collection of African-American improvisational quilts. Contrasting color and values of fabrics, as well as contrasting patterns, are often juxtaposed in a single quilt with the intent of making the whole quilt "show up."

Score for Showing Up

This score invites you first to evaluate and identify a personal lexicon of improvisational patchwork techniques and shapes and then juxtapose two or more of them into a single composition. It also introduces the technique for Natural Shaping of a Quilt Top (page 152).

Draw on the entire vocabulary of skills learned from this book and from your existing knowledge base to create a composition populated with a complex cast of characters or narratives. How do they relate? How do they "show up" and occupy the space of the quilt in harmony and in conflict? How do their similarities and differences work together to create a complex community and an interesting story?

"How I start to make a quilt, all I do is start sewing, and it just comes to me. No pattern. I usually don't use a pattern, only my mind."

—Loraine Pettway, from
The Quilts of Gee's Bend

step 1. identify your lexicon of shapes and methods

Throughout the previous scores in this chapter, you have been introduced to several different improvisational techniques and methods: Ruler-Free Strip Piecing (page 127), simple patchwork doodles (page 50), Floating Squares (page 24), block repetitions (page 70), Rhythmic Grids (page 58), Layered Curves (page 78), Bias Strip Piecing on the Curve (page 140), and Wedge Strip Piecing on the Curve (page 146). Add to this list any techniques and shapes previously learned and mastered, for example, paper-pieced hexagons, reverse-appliqué, foundational piecing, scrap quilting, or Log Cabins.

step 2. evaluate works in progress

If you, like most quilters I know, have a stash of works in progress, or WIPs, whip them out and take inventory. With each one consider the reasons you stopped working on the project. Have you gained any new pieces of information or experience that will move the project toward completion? Apply the Evaluation Exercise on page 20 and notice if this sparks a different way of seeing the WIP. Identify any WIPs you might want to consider incorporating into your combo quilt.

step 3. juxtapose your composition

Draw from the patchwork methods listed in Step 1 and your shelved WIPs to combine non-congruent large sections of patchwork into a single composition.

If you have readymade sections from a WIP, throw them up on your design wall or spread them out on a clean floor in different juxtapositions. Imagine you are auditioning a cast of characters. How do they interact, clash, and coincide?

Audition sections of WIPs with newly created patchwork based on your lexicon of shapes and methods. Let the variety of components speak to you. When an arrangement feels right or risky, go ahead and begin piecing the composition in a flexible way, committing to one step at a time.

If you have no previously pieced scraps to start with, choose one technique or shape and work with it for as long as you please and then switch to a different mode of patchwork. Pause to carefully look with fresh eyes at what's emerging on your design wall. If a composition doesn't emerge spontaneously or flow organically, you can always narrow your composition limits and superimpose a simple geometric structure for your composition, for example a square unequally bordered by a different pattern, and bordered again by a third.

step 4. evaluate your experience and results

Apply the Evaluation Exercise on page 20, after making your quilt top to assess what you've learned from the experience and to identify your next steps.

step 5. shape your finished quilt top

You may have noticed that improvisational ruler-free patchwork develops a final shape of its own. The quilt top can be squared off, or it can be naturally shaped, or some combination of both. To learn how, follow the Natural Shaping of a Quilt Top technique on page 152.

design considerations
GOING BIMODAL

Not only did Eli Leon recognize how African-American quilt makers juxtaposed contrasting colors and patterns in a single quilt, he noticed how they deliberately juxtaposed fixed patterning and flexible patterning in their compositions. He called this effortless and unceremonious movement between fixed and flexible modes of patterning "bimodal."

If you have some fixed-pattern blocks in your work-in-progress pile, try working the same block with flexible patterning by applying some of the approaches outlined in the Score for Modern Block Improv on page 70. Juxtapose the fixed blocks and the flexible blocks in the same quilt and go bimodal.

IT OFTEN HAPPENS THAT I CREATE patchwork for a composition that doesn't pan out, and that patchwork later becomes the beautiful, yet unexpected, centerpiece in another quilt. That is exactly how my Showing Up quilt (page 104) came into being. Whenever this happens, I'm reminded that the creative process is nonlinear and even "failures" are not wasted effort but the worthy steppingstones of transformation.

WORK IN PROGRESS: When I was working on my Layered Curve compositions (page 78), I followed through on an idea to make rectangular layered curve sections **(a)** to use as a border for the small and chaotic multiple-curve composition. **(b)** The idea didn't work, so I scrapped it.

However, I still loved the sections and had a mind to use them elsewhere. Eventually I threw them back on my design wall and arranged them not as a border but in a central mass. **(c)**

I also had some odd bits of strip sections in my pieced-scrap bin. At some point, the idea of juxtaposing the mass of layered curve sections with strip-pieced sections popped into my head. Once that happened, constructing the quilt was a breeze. **(d, e)**

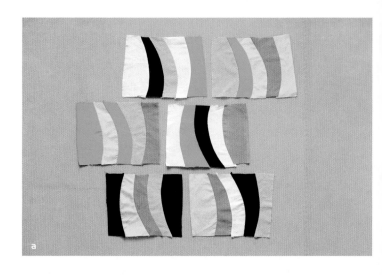

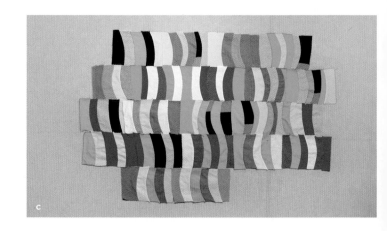

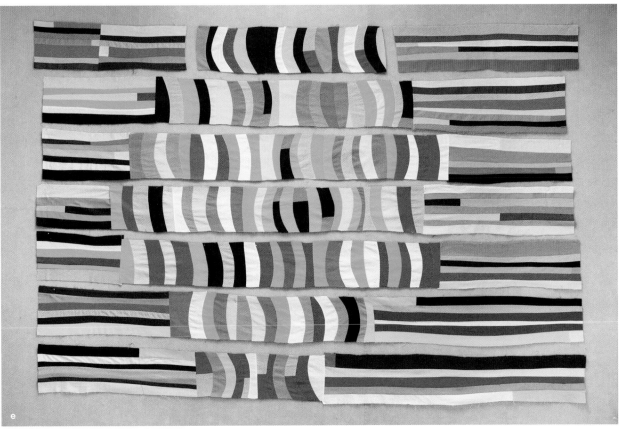

SCORE #10: Showing Up

The contributor quilts in this gallery are culled from quilts made for other scores because they juxtaposed more than one patchwork approach.

Stacey Sharman's quilt (far right) and Sarah Fielke's quilt (near right, bottom) are Modern Block Improv (page 70) interpretations. However, they both also subtly juxtaposed intervals of strip piecing with their flying geese repetitions. These are great examples of two authentic voices showing up through the same score.

Heather Kojan's quilt (near right, top) is a Bias Strip Petals (page 86) interpretation. It effectively juxtaposes strip-pieced petal centers with curved strip-pieced rings around the petals to create a fresh and fun lineup of surfboard shapes that show up and stand up!

Heather Kojan   Stacey Sharman
Sarah Fielke

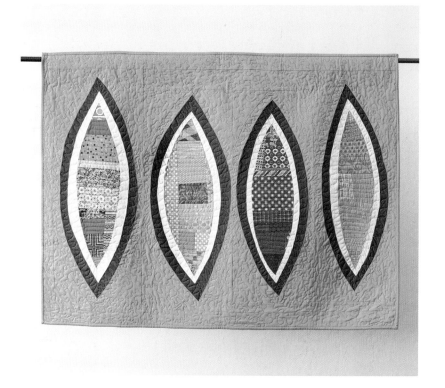

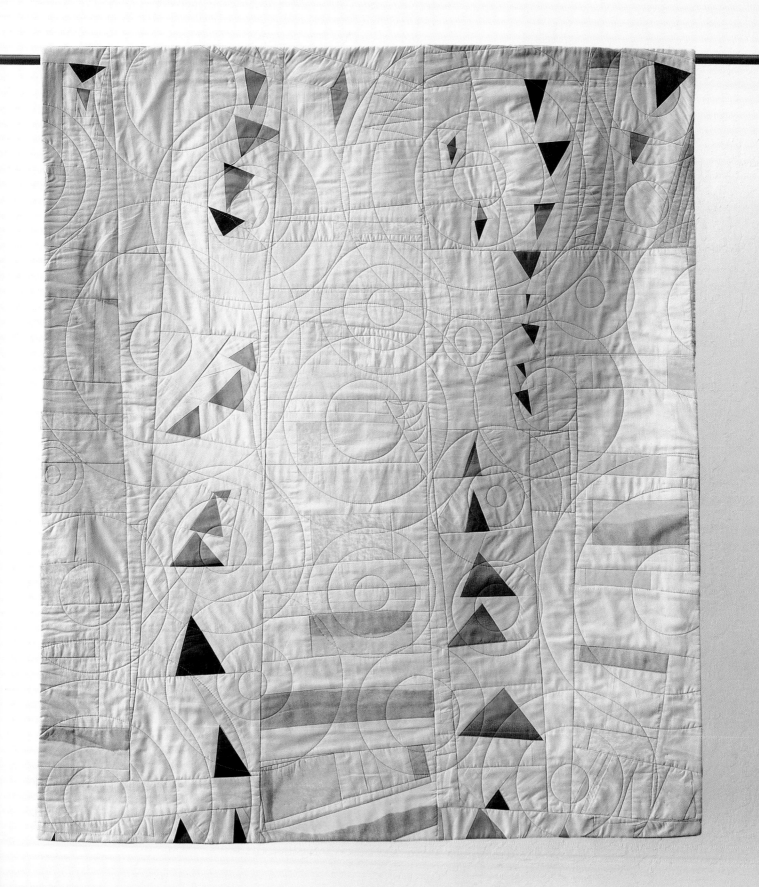

3

Exploring Color

Color Scores

While my mother wasn't a seamstress, she was a bold woman when it came to color in the home. I can't remember a plain white wall in any of the places we lived during my childhood, but I have a vivid memory of our living room in the '70s: dark avocado shag carpet, gold velvet sofa, and rust brocade armchair, with my mother standing in the middle of it all wearing electric blue hip-hugger bellbottoms with a white belt and a silver buckle. Now that's a color palette! I have no doubt that my education in color began with my childhood experiences.

Color plays a major role in every quilt. The passion for color and imagining combinations of color is a driving force for many of us who make and collect quilts. Even those who are most familiar and comfortable with following a fixed pattern have the desire to choose their own colors and fabrics to make the quilt their own. For many, it's their first exposure to improvisation.

The project scores in this book give some opportunity for you to consider your own color preferences. For this chapter, I've written two scores specifically for exploring color. The first is an overview of several aspects of color and models how limits can be defined for any aspect to explore it further. The second is an example of a score written to explore just one aspect of color, hue, as it affects mood. In both of these scores, you can create string sheets, as you did in the Strings project score (page 32). Once you've made a few string sheets, try applying color limits to all of the scores in this book.

a *Hue and Neutral Hues: Rainbow hues pop next to neutrals.*

b *Value: Shades of green matched to a gray scale.*

c *Temperature: Cool and warm yellows and blues.*

Aspects of Color

There are plenty of design books that explain color theory, but the best way to learn about color is through experience. Whenever we make choices, we are defining parameters and setting limits. I hope the following score will help you understand different aspects of color and support the exploration of new color territories.

step 1. review the various aspects of color

Here are some basic aspects of color as I understand them. As you read through them, pay attention to what resonates with your experiences working with color. What would you add or change?

✕ Hue is the aspect of color referred to by color names—reds, oranges, yellows, blues, greens, violets, and everything in between. Use the aspect of hue to define the mood of a quilt (explore mood further in the score on page 118). **(a)**

✕ Neutral hues appear to be devoid of color and commonly include variations of black, white, gray, and beige. They often have undertones of pure hues, such as purplish gray or rosy beige. Pure hues will appear more vivid when combined with neutrals. **(a)**

✕ Value is the aspect of color that ranges from light to dark on the gray scale. Every hue has a value; the values of the hue green range from light green to dark green. The underlying experience of value has more of an impact on how patterns stand out than any other aspect of color. Squinting at a color combination is helpful in determining values. **(b)**

✕ Temperature is a more subtle aspect of color hue that ranges from cool to warm. Yellow, orange, and red are considered warm hues. Green, blue, and purple are considered cool. Temperature is always relative; a blue that leans toward green is considered warm, and a blue that leans toward purple is considered cool. Consider the relationship of temperature between your choices for a more sophisticated color palette. **(c)**

✕ Intensity is the aspect of color that measures the saturation, brightness, luminosity, or the force of the color. Intensity is a trickster and plays a fascinating role in the way patterns both show up and blend. A bright or intense yellow has the same value as a pale blue. A bright orange has the same value as a medium gray. The intensity of a bright yellow or orange when combined in a pattern with pale blue or medium gray, respectively, causes the pattern to stand out, in spite of the fact that their values merge when viewed on a scale from light to dark. **(d)**

d *Intensity: Orange/yellow pop next to gray/blue of equal value.*

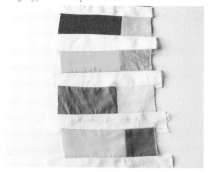

e *Afterimage: Paired after image colors.*

f *High Impact: Hues and values contrast.*

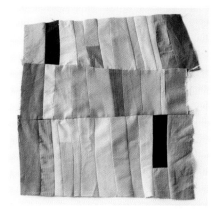

g *Low Volume: Hues and values blend.*

✖ **Afterimage** is an internal experience of color. It is an illusion of inverted or contrasting color that appears briefly after staring at an actual color for a few seconds. To determine the afterimage color of any color, place the color on a white background and stare at it for ten to twenty seconds. Shift your eyes to a blank white background. The afterimage color will appear briefly before it gradually fades away. Like value, the effects of afterimage color have an underlying, or less conscious, impact on the way people experience color. Combine opposing afterimage colors to make patterns reverberate and pop. **(e)**

✖ **High-impact** color combinations juxtapose light and dark values, low and high intensity, and afterimage oppositions. High-impact combinations show up and result in patterns that stand out. **(f)**

✖ **Low-volume** color combinations are similar in hue and value and are low intensity. Low-volume combinations result in patterns that blend together and read as a unified color field. **(g)**

step 2. define aspect ranges to test color preferences

As you choose fabrics based on their color aspects, experiment with less appealing or unlikely combinations to test the limits of what you know about color. For instance, curate what you consider to be a perfectly color-coordinated group of fabrics, then add one fabric that you absolutely hate and would never choose to include. If you typically choose fabrics that are in the light-value, low-intensity range, notice how the mix changes when you add a few fabrics in the light-value, high-intensity range or the dark-value, high-intensity range. When in doubt, choose what scares you!

step 3. apply your choices to a pattern

Explore ambitious color parameters without risking the outcome of an entire quilt project by employing your choices to create a series of string sheets as described on pages 34–35. The string sheets will allow you to quickly see how the color limits you set play out. Keep the string sheets as reference or store them in your pieced scrap bin for use later.

step 4. evaluate your experience and results

Apply the Evaluation Exercise (page 20) after making each sheet to assess what you've learned from the experience and to define your next color exploration.

COLOR SCORES

Moods of Color

Ever since my fascination with mood rings when I was a kid in the '70s, I've been drawn to the symbolic, cultural, and emotional aspects of color. Color perception and our emotional responses to color, particularly the aspect of hue, are shaped through our personal experience and memories, as well as our cultural environment. Establishing a personal mood color chart and harnessing your emotional energy is an intuitive way to discover new color frontiers. In the following score, you'll become more aware of your emotional connection to color and how to use that awareness to create a sense of mood in your quilts.

> "I like to sew all kinds of colors together and see what I can come up with."
> —Irene Bankhead from
> *Accidentally on Purpose* by Eli Leon

step 1. review mood associations with hue

Pay attention to what resonates as you review this list of color hues and the range of emotional mind states often associated with them.

Black: harassed, oppressed, emptiness, void, mystery, allure, independent, strength

Gray: anxious, strained, depressed, perseverance, patience, reflection

Amber-gold: nervous, mixed emotions, unsettled, warm, rich

Lime green: excited, anticipation, new growth, perceptive, motivated

Green: growth, abundance, gratitude, contentment, envy, jealousy

Blue-green: dynamic, refreshed, tranquil, patience, cool, fussy, egocentric

Blue: calm, lovable, sincerity, peace, tranquility, faith, trust, truthful, sad, arrogant

Dark blue: deeply happy, love, romance, integrity, intuition, knowledge, fantasy

White: cold, confused, bored, vacant, bare, peace, innocence, purity, open, faith

Brown: earth, comforting, nurturing, grounded, cozy, secure, elegant, fertile, humble

Bronze: jitters, anticipation, restless

Yellow: imaginative, cheerful, curious, self-assured, productive

Orange: stimulating, creative, daring, joy, enthusiasm, busy, bright

Red: excited, energized, adventurous, passion, courage, power, desire, anger

Pink: fear, vulnerable, uncertain, love, affection, harmony, gentleness

Purple: sensual, clarity, wisdom, spirituality, passion, mystical, regal

Make a color wheel of fabrics and consider the moods associated with each hue.

step 2. organize your fabrics by color

Organize your collection of fabrics by color. Use solids, and if you want to include prints, organize them by their dominant color. Display them on a table so they are in your field of vision. You don't have to make a color wheel with them, but you can if you want! Notice if you have a full range of colors, and if not, consider why that might be. Next time you are fabric shopping, consider supplementing your stash with colors you are missing.

step 3. chart your emotional response to color

From a centered meditative place, scan the range of colors in your field of vision to see what associations arise. Does blue make you sad? Relaxed? Intuitive? Why? Take some time to write down your emotional responses and assign a loose list of memories and emotional associations for each color. If you like, use the Centering Exercise on page 47.

step 4. use your mood color chart to choose fabrics

The colors corresponding to my moods on one particular day.

I often lead students through a centering exercise at the beginning of my workshops right before they choose fabrics. These students overwhelmingly report that they chose fabric combinations they had never worked with before or that were very different from what they had in mind going into the exercise.

At the beginning of a work session, identify the unique mix of emotions that are with you in the present moment. Once you become aware of what you are feeling, invite your emotions to co-create with you. Often your emotions will be mixed. Accept them all without judging. Welcome them into the studio to help you choose your fabrics for the day. Do this intuitively and spontaneously, or use your mood color chart as a guide to pick colors that correspond with the emotions you've identified. On the day of the final photo shoot for this book, I was feeling curious, creative, active, tired, nervous, busy, efficient, grounded, and hopeful, and I chose the colors at left to correspond with my emotions.

step 5. apply your choices to a pattern

Chart your emotions over the course of several studio sessions by creating a string sheet, as outlined on pages 34–35, from your choices for each session. These string sheets can be filed in your pieced scrap bin for later use or put together in a single composition. Or apply your choices to any of the flexible patterns outlined in the project score chapters in this book.

step 6. evaluate your experience and outcomes

Apply the Evaluation Exercise (page 20) after making each mood color string sheet to assess what you've learned and to clarify your shifting emotional responses to color.

As you continue to engage with the quilt project scores, apply either of these methods for exploring color to choose your fabrics.

Patchwork Techniques

4

EQUALIZING PATCHWORK SECTIONS

Equalizing patchwork sections can be done in two ways: by cutting the longer fabric to match the shorter piece or by adding to the shorter piece to match the longer piece. My preference is to add whenever possible to keep the patchwork expansive.

1 Place two different-sized squares alongside each other.

2 Obviously, the adjacent edges are unequal. So in order to equalize the edges before sewing the seam, stitch a piece of filler fabric along one edge of the smaller square to bring it up in size to match the larger square.

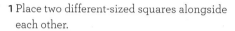

3 Since you are not measuring, you may overshoot the mark. Simply trim your filler fabric to match the length of the square to which it is joined.

4 Now sew the smaller square with filler to the larger square.

5 Trim off the excess filler once again.

The Improv Handbook for Modern Quilters

122

Floating Squares quilt, detail, page 24.

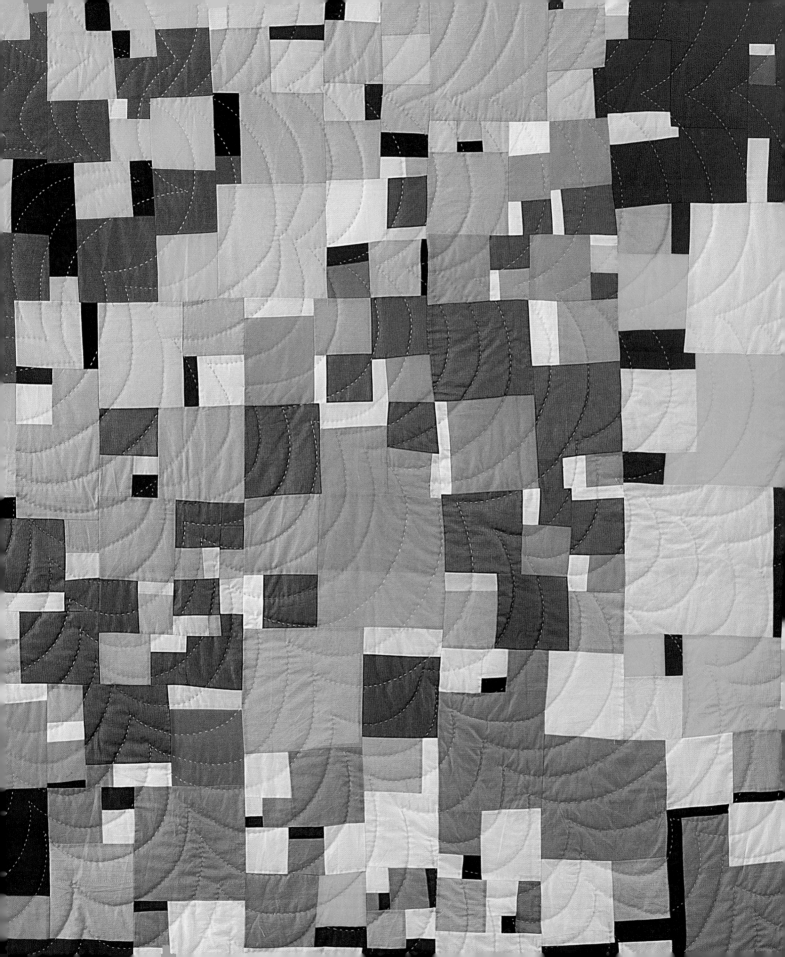

RULER-FREE PATCHWORK

This is the fundamental ruler-free technique for joining any two sections of equal length without using a ruler or template. Your freely cut piecing line can be relatively straight, slope at an angle, or follow a gentle curve. That is the beauty of ruler-free patchwork.

1 Any two sections can easily be joined without using a ruler or template. It's most helpful to join two sections that are already the same length.

2 Overlap the sections, right sides up, along the edge you wish to join so that there are no spaces exposed. Cut through both layers using either a rotary cutter and mat or a scissors.

3 Expose the excess that's been trimmed away (the blue strip), and discard it.

4 Once the edges are trimmed to match, flip one section over on the other, with right sides facing and edges even.

5 I don't bother pinning, but do so according to your skill and comfort level.

6 Stitch along the edges, leaving a ¼" (6 mm) seam allowance. Press seams according to your preference or in the best way for reducing bulk.

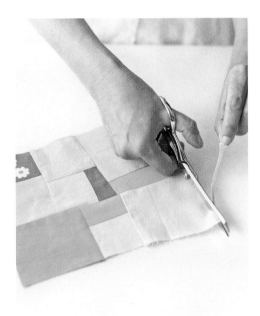

7 Trim after joining sections. Or if you prefer, leave sections untrimmed for more flexibility with joining options and seam shaping down the road.

Patchwork Doodle quilt, detail, page 50.

CUTTING FROM YOUR CORE

Feel your feet on the ground and follow the energy as it moves up through the ground into your core center then out through your shoulders, arms, wrists, and hand as you cut without a ruler or template. Experiment with the way you cut strips. Cut wavier or straighter strips. Cut with scissors or with a rotary cutter. When you notice your mind wandering, bring it back gently to the task of cutting. What happens to your line when you cut with your full attention?

1 I prefer to cut strips from selvage to selvage. Your strips can be any width as long as they are all the same length. If a piece of fabric does not meet the target length, sew another fabric onto the end before cutting it into the strips.

2 Whether using scissors or a rotary cutter, cut your strips without a ruler from end to end. Strips don't have to be perfectly straight. Be centered, and pay attention as you cut and your signature line will emerge.

3 Cut with assurance and presence.

4 Once your strips are cut, organize them by placing the strips for each string sheet in its own pile, bag, or box.

RULER-FREE STRIP PIECING

Use this technique to make string sheets that can be used whole, cut into cross-strips or any shape for patchwork and other sewing projects, or to explore the different aspects of color as described on page 116. Joining strips to make a string sheet is a meditative process that can jump-start your creative flow.

1 Join hand-cut strips, ignoring any irregularities. Instead, align any unevenly cut edges as you sew a ¼" (6-mm) seam allowance just as you would if they were cut to match with a ruler.

2 Add individual strips or batches of strips to both sides of the string sheet to counter a tendency for the sheet to curve. If you like the curving effect, add strips to just one side.

3 Soften the seams with steam and press from the center out.

4 Allow seams to press in the direction they prefer. This enhances the irregularities of your line. Press seams in one direction to decrease the irregularities.

5 Since the strips were not cut to match, you may notice bubbles of excess fabric. Slice through bubbles as you cut the string sheet into shapes or filler pieces.

PATCHWORK TECHNIQUES

DARTING

With ruler-free patchwork, sometimes a wobble will develop along the edge so the piece doesn't lie flat. This typically happens when the edges of two pieces of patchwork are not cut to match before seaming. No worries—take a dart to remove the distortion with barely a trace.

1 Take a dart as soon as you notice a wobble of excess fabric. If left unchecked the distortion will grow.

2 Spread the patchwork out and gently manipulate the fabric to find where the excess fabric naturally wants to gather.

3 Once you find the best place to take the dart, finger press the excess fabric into place. Here the dart is forming along the seam line.

4 Pin the dart in place, and iron if necessary to create a strong crease.

5 Remove the pins and, with the wrong side up, sew exactly along the crease line.

6 Here is the seam side.

7 From the right side, the dart along the seam is invisible and the piece now lies flat. Trim excess fabric from the back if necessary.

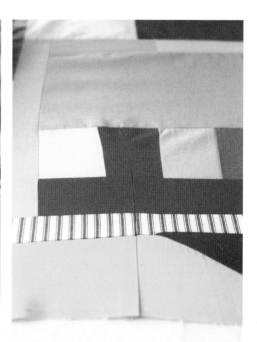

8 Sometimes a wobble may occur in the middle of the quilt or across seam lines. As above, follow the contours of the wobble or bubble and gently finger press it into a dart and pin in place.

9 Flip and sew following the crease line of the dart across seam lines. If a dart falls in the middle of the quilt, the crease line will taper at both ends.

10 Once sewn and pressed, the dart will go unnoticed in the context of the entire quilt. If it is a tricky wobble that meanders or it's in the center of your patchwork and hard to reach by machine, it may be easier to fold and pin the dart in place and appliqué it by hand. See the technique Hand Appliquéing for Large Shapes on page 150.

RULER-FREE PATCHWORK WITH LARGE SECTIONS

Joining large sections of patchwork without a ruler follows the same basic procedure outlined in the Ruler-Free Patchwork technique for joining smaller units (page 124). The only difference is that you will use your scissors, chalk, and pins to make a well-fit and flat seam.

1 Lay the sections to be joined on a large horizontal surface, side by side and right sides up.

2 Layer the sections, with the edge you want your seam to follow on top of the other edge. Mark the edge of the top layer on the bottom layer with a piece of chalk.

3 Cut along the chalk line with sharp scissors and discard the excess.

4 Butt the two matching sections together and mark across the seam line at regular intervals.

5 Flip right sides together, and pin at the matching chalk lines. Add more pins between the marked lines as necessary to hold the sections together comfortably.

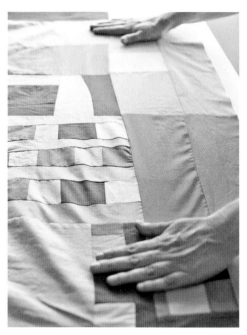

6 Sew with a ¼" (6-mm) seam allowance, removing each pin right before you reach it. Press your selected seam. Your patchwork should lie flat. Slight irregularities will disappear with quilting. Remove noticeable bubbles with the Darting technique, page 128.

Improv Round Robin quilt, detail, page 40.

APPROXIMATE MEASURING

This technique is a refinement of Ruler-Free Patchwork (page 124) that allows you to match cross seams approximately, if not almost perfectly. All it requires is that you rely on your eye to consider the ¼" (6 mm) seam allowance before trimming sections to match. The more you measure by eye the closer you will get to "perfect"—if that is your goal.

1 Lay out the primary section of patchwork. Prepare two or more smaller units of patchwork to be added to the primary section.

2 Align the first unit with the edge of the primary section. Layer the second unit on top of the first so that its edge aligns next to and approximately ¼" (6 mm) beyond the cross seam of the primary section being matched.

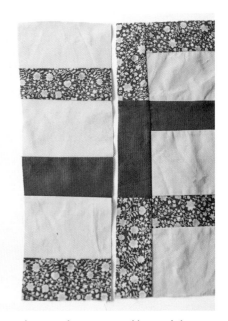

3 Cut the edges of the two smaller units as they lay. Flip right sides together and sew.

4 Continue to measure by eye to align, layer, cut, and sew segment by segment, always allowing an extra ¼" (6 mm) for the seam allowance on the segment being built.

5 Once the joined units extend beyond the primary section, follow the techniques for Equalizing Patchwork Sections (page 122) and Ruler-Free Patchwork (page 124) to make sure the seam edges are cut to match.

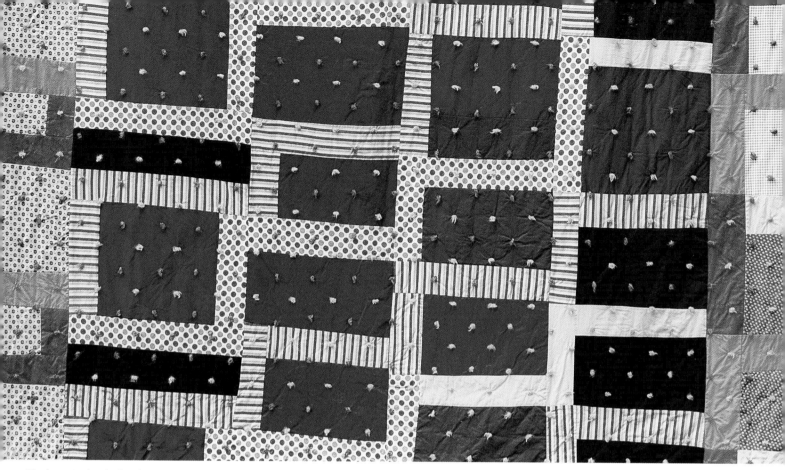

Rhythmic Grid quilt, detail, page 58.

6 Flip right sides together, match edges, pin at seam intersections, and sew.

7 Seams may not match perfectly, but they will match approximately.

8 Enjoy the imperfections. They make your quilt and you more interesting!

PATCHWORK TECHNIQUES

NATURAL SHAPING

As you create units and build sections, resist the urge to square them off with a ruler or even by eye. Instead, allow your sections to remain in their natural shapes. Piecing with natural shapes will add a more organic flow and rhythm to your composition.

 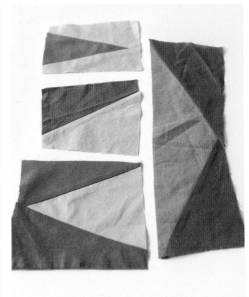

1 Trim off any overhanging bits of fabric from units and sections to define their natural shapes.

2 By not squaring off but preserving the natural shape of your units there will be more opportunities to Make Do (see Design Consideration on page 67). More often than not, naturally shaped units will fit together like pieces of a puzzle.

PATCHWORK PUZZLE

The composition approach of moving premade units around like puzzle pieces to find natural fits and bleeds is an alternative to the responsive build-as-you-go approach used for the Patchwork Doodle (page 50), Improv Round Robin (page 40), and Rhythmic Grid (page 58) quilts. The puzzle approach requires that you make do with what you have and let the patchwork be your guide.

For this technique, be selective and use the units that please you. You don't need to use every unit in your final composition.

1 Spontaneously arrange and rearrange the units on a design wall or flat surface. Pause and pay attention to relationships between arrangements. Look for natural fits—places where the shapes of your units fit together naturally like puzzle pieces. In this photo, the top unit is not a natural fit.

Modern Block Improv quilt, detail, page 70.

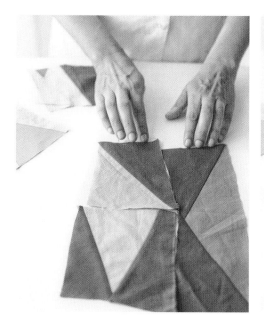

2 But with a quarter turn, the top unit fits in place like a puzzle piece without trimming.

3 Look for bleeds, places where color, value, shape, or cross lines meet to blur the seam line between sections, just as a puzzle's image will bleed beyond the borders of the puzzle pieces. By moving the right piece in Step 2 to the other side, the lighter values bleed together to form a more interesting shape. Avoid inset seams as much as possible. However, if you have the skill set, take on tricky piecing situations as an opportunity to innovate.

TEMPLATE-FREE LAYERED CURVE PATCHWORK

This is the basic technique for cutting and sewing curves without a template. Keep in mind that each time you cut and sew a curve the starting size of your sections or blocks will decrease by ½" (12 mm) due to seam allowances.

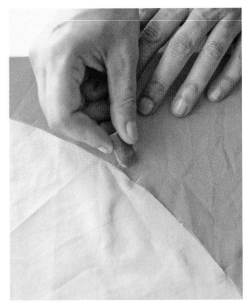

1 Start with two or more units approximately the same size and layer them right sides up into a stack.

2 Cut a curve through all the layers of the stack.

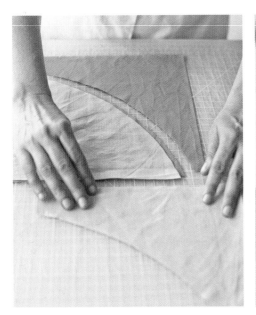

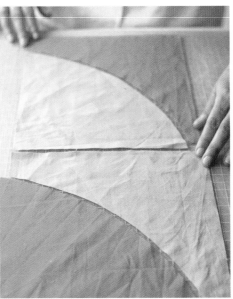

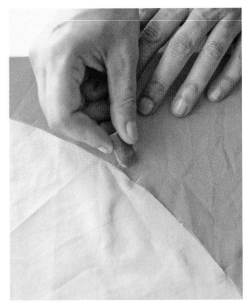

3 Keeping right sides up, mix and match the convex and concave pieces.

4 The convex pieces curve outward, like the outer edge of a circle; the concave pieces round inward, like the inside of a bowl.

5 Use chalk to mark across the arc of the curve at regular intervals.

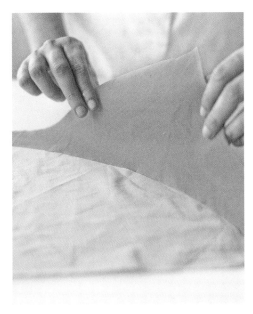

6 Flip right sides together with the concave curve on top.

7 Starting from the center out, match marks and pin.

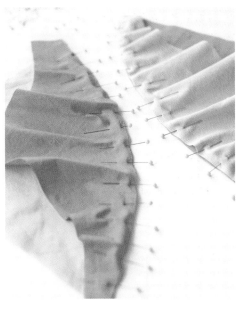

8 Add more pins as necessary, slightly contracting the concave edge of the curve to fit the convex edge.

9 Notice how the concave edge is gathered when pinned and the convex edge is smooth. I prefer to sew the seam with the gathered concave side up.

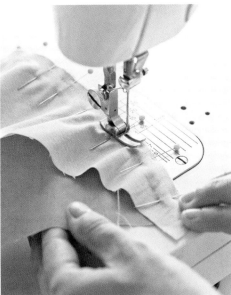

10 Slowly and carefully sew a ¼" (6-mm) seam, removing each pin right before you reach it. Do not machine stitch over pins.

11 Press seams to one side. The finished curve should lie flat. The shallower the curve, the easier it will be to sew.

PATCHWORK TECHNIQUES

RULER-FREE
CONTINUOUS BIAS STRIPS

Use this technique to create continuous bias strips anywhere from 1" to 4" (2.5 cm to 10 cm) wide for strip piecing on the curve. Unlike making continuous bias binding, there is no need to mark cutting lines with a ruler!

1 Begin with a large square of fabric of any size.

2 Fold the square diagonally and cut along the fold line.

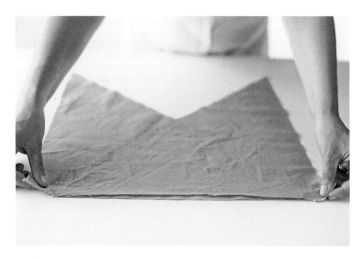

3 Align cross grain or selvage edges with right sides together. The diagonal bias edge will create a *V* in the center.

4 Sew a ¼" (6 mm) seam and press open. The two joined triangles will now be in the shape of a parallelogram.

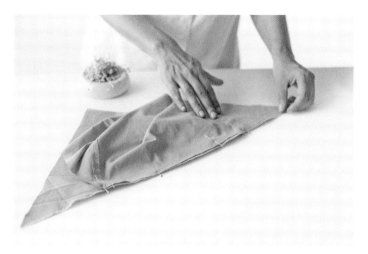

5 Bring together the two edges perpendicular to the first seam line, which will be the non-bias edges, to form a tube. Offset the edges by the approximate width of your strip and pin in place.

6 Sew a ¼" (6 mm) seam and press open. You will now have a tube with two overhanging edges.

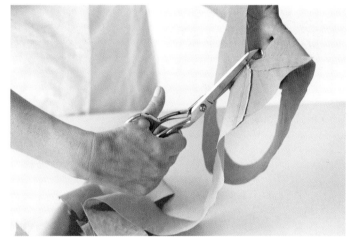

7 Begin cutting the continuous bias strip at one of the overlapped edges, measuring by eye.

8 Once started, I place my arm through the tube and continue cutting the strip to the end. Keep the width consistent or gradually increase and decrease the width as you cut.

technique

BIAS STRIP PIECING ON THE CURVE

When piecing bias strips on the curve, it is helpful to imagine manipulating the spaces between the warp and weft threads by easing—stretching the base curve and contracting the strip—as you sew. Mastering this technique may require some trial and error in order to develop a feel for how much stretch is required along the arc of the curve. These steps explain how to add the series of bias strips along the convex curves on petal shapes, as on the Bias Strip Petals quilt (pages 86–94).

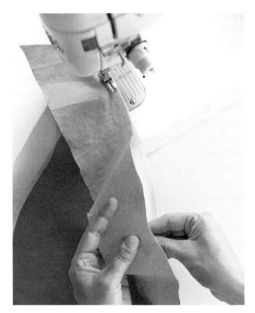

1 I prefer to attach strips with the curved edge (the petal) on the bottom and the strip on top. As you sew, gently stretch the petal edge while holding the bias strip loosely so that it doesn't stretch.

2 The amount of stretch required along the arc of the curve varies. Stretch the petal less or not at all at the ends and more toward the center.

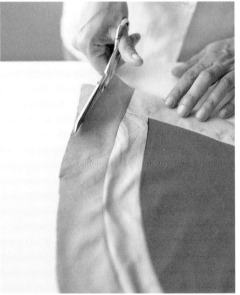

3 Notice how the bias strip looks gathered along the deepest arc of the curve.

4 Give the newly attached strip a good stretch to help expand the space between warp and weft. Steam-press the seam away from the center after adding each strip. Trim off the bias-strip excess.

5 Shape the arc of the curve by trimming the edge of the newly added strip before sewing the next strip, or leave the strips in their natural shape.

Bias Strip Petals quilt detail, page 86

technique

DARTING ALONG THE CURVE

Bias-strip piecing on the curve is tricky. If bubbles of excess fabric appear along the curve, and keep the patchwork from laying flat, just take a dart along the seam to remedy the problem.

1 Gently flatten the petal and press the bubble toward the seam where it naturally wants to gather.

2 Press the excess fabric forward of the original seam along the line of the curve.

3 Finger press and pin the dart in place. The original seam should be pressed away from the direction of the dart and the dart seam pressed forward of the original seam.

4 Press with a steam iron as you remove the pins to get a clean sharp crease where the dart is pressed forward from the original seam.

5 When the fabric is turned over there will be a crease line visible just in front of the original seam line following the line of the curve.

6 On the wrong side, carefully re-sew the seam line by stitching directly on the darted crease line from start to finish.

7 Open and press. If the excess fabric doesn't dart cleanly along the seam line, or it's in a very inaccessible place in the center of your patchwork, it might be easier to finger press and sew the dart by hand using an appliqué stitch (page 150).

DARTING ACROSS
THE CURVE

Use this technique when your curved patchwork has a wobble. Wobbles on the curve occur when the base curved section has been overstretched while attaching the bias strip. The technique is much the same as the Darting technique on page 128.

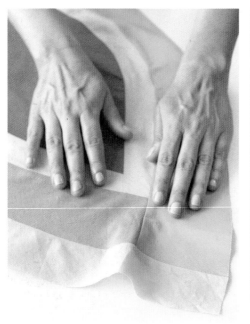

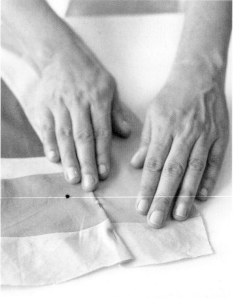

1 Spread the patchwork flat and gently manipulate the excess fabric to find the most natural lay of the wobble. It may or may not line up with a cross seam.

2 Once you find the best place to take the dart, fold the fabric and finger press, pin, then iron the dart if necessary to create a strong crease.

3 Remove the pins and with the wrong side up, sew exactly along the crease line. From the top, a dart along a cross seam will be invisible; however, there may be a slight jag in the patchwork when the dart falls across the curve but not along a cross seam. No worries—this will add interest or go unnoticed.

TRIMMING THE CURVE

Use this technique when the bias strip you attached curls along the arc of the curve. Curling occurs when the base section wasn't stretched enough during sewing, most often when attaching wide bias strips.

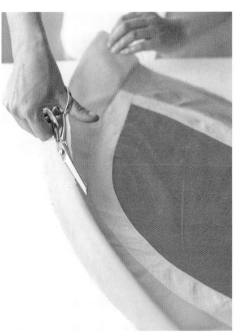

1 Stretch the curling strip by hand along the outer edge and press. If a curl persists, flatten the base petal so that the curled edge becomes distinct.

2 Simply trim the strip along the edge of the curl to remove the curling fabric. Give the new outer edge a good stretch before ironing to help the space between warp and weft expand so that the fabric will lie flat.

WEDGE STRIP
PIECING ON THE CURVE

The wedged curve sections created with this simple technique can be used whole in your compositions or treated as base material to layer and cut into multiple curves or even other shapes.

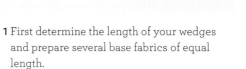

1 First determine the length of your wedges and prepare several base fabrics of equal length.

2 Stack and cut base fabrics mindfully into wedges, or cut wedges one by one. The length of the base fabrics must be the same but the widths can vary.

3 Continue to cut wedges, making sure one end is wider than the other.

4 Once the wedges have been cut, choose them spontaneously. Align the wide ends of the wedges at the top to form a curve.

5 Sew wedges together aligning seam edges, even if they are not cut to fit, with a ¼" (6-mm) seam allowance. Press.

6 Create *S*-curves, reversing the direction of the curve, by aligning the narrow ends of the wedges at the top.

EQUALIZING AND JOINING CURVE SECTIONS

The basic principles used to join straight-edged patchwork introduced in Equalizing Patchwork Sections (page 122) and Ruler-Free Patchwork (page 124) apply to curve patchwork, too. The only difference is that joining curves requires more skill and practice.

1 When joining two curve sections together of unequal length, overlap them right sides up in an arrangement of your choice to amply determine how much filler fabric you will need.

2 Arrange the filler fabric to extend the shorter of the two curved sections to equal the length of the longer section. Determine how much to extend the breadth of the filler fabric so the curve extends to the outer edge in a graceful manner.

3 Cut the filler fabric to match the end of the shorter curve section and sew it in place.

4 With the two sections now equal in length, overlap the sections again with right sides facing up. Trim the excess filler as needed by extending the natural line of the piece it's being attached to.

5 Cut the curve to be sewn through both sections, following the edge of the section on top.

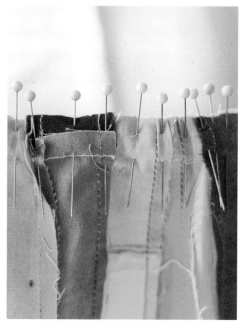

6 Remove the trimmed edges and save for possible use later in the composition. The two pieces should be like yin to yang.

7 Mark perpendicular lines across the cut curve with chalk in several places. Flip right sides together, matching the chalk lines.

8 Ease in the fabric as you pin on the concave side of the curve. Place the pins perpendicular to and about ¼" (6 mm) in from the edge. The tighter the curve, the more pins you will need. I usually pin every edge seam on both curves.

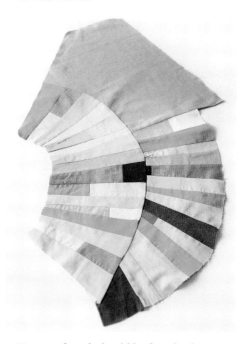

9 Notice how the concave side is ruffled. Sew ¼" (6 mm) in from the edge along the pin line, removing the pins just before you reach them.

10 Hover and steam and then press seams to one side. Flip the piece over and press on the front.

11 Your patchwork should lie flat. If it doesn't, use the Darting technique (page 144) to remove any unintended wobbles.

PATCHWORK TECHNIQUES

HAND APPLIQUÉING FOR LARGE SHAPES

Sometimes I find it easier to hand appliqué tricky darts and sharp curves into place rather than joining them by machine. I welcome the opportunity to slow my process down for handwork when it arises.

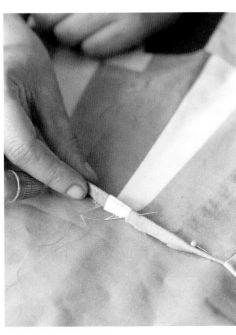

1 To stabilize the edge of the piece that is going to be on top, machine stitch ¼" (6 mm) from the edge along the curve. This line of stitching (called stay stitching), keeps the edge of the fabric from stretching as you appliqué it to the bottom piece, and it serves as a guideline for turning the edge under.

2 Position the sections you are joining with right sides facing up. Place the top section so that it overlaps the bottom section by at least ¼" (6 mm).

3 Turn the edge under at the stay stitch. Finger press the fold and pin in place. Choose a neutral thread color that blends with the colors of the section on top.

4 Begin hand stitching the turned under edge in place along the straightest edge, and working from right to left, bring the needle up from the underside, through the fold of the top piece to hide the thread knot.

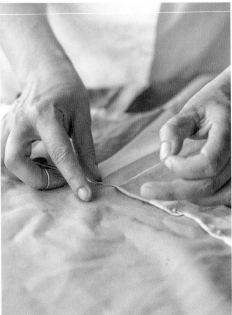

5 Bring the needle up at an angle through the background fabric and through the fold of the appliqué edge ⅛" to ¼" (3 mm to 6 mm) beyond the previous stitch.

6 Pull the thread taut, but not tight, to secure the seam smoothly without puckers.

7 Once again insert the needle into the background fabric slightly beyond the previous stitch. I use a thimble on my middle finger to push the needle through both layers at once.

8 After appliquéing the edge of the top fabric in place, remove the pins.

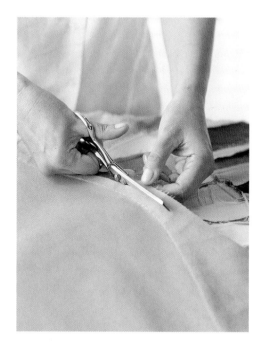

9 Flip to the back side of your quilt top, and carefully trim the excess fabric ¼" (6 mm) from the hand stitching line. Steam press.

Showing Up quilt, detail, page 104.

NATURAL SHAPING OF A QUILT TOP

The typical way to "square off" a quilt top is to use a ruler to cut the edges of the quilt down to precise 90° angles. For a less rigid squaring off, build the quilt out by eye to reach your approximate target size and shape.

1 Aid your eye by drawing a chalk outline of the target size for your quilt on your design wall or by taping off the target size on a horizontal surface with blue painter's tape.

2 Once you've reached or surpassed your goal size, trim away any patchwork that overhangs the target line using scissors. Or, as in the image above, let the natural shape of your quilt top stand by trimming only slightly to clean up rough edges before quilting and binding.

5 Finishing Techniques

Finishing

Once your improv quilt top is complete, it's time to make it into a quilt. Here I share my favorite techniques for basting, quilting, and binding quilts.

Quilt Construction

A quilt is technically three layers: the top, the batting (or filling), and the back. Following are some of your options for your quilt batting and backing.

BATTING

Batting is available in polyester, cotton, wool, and mixtures of these. Look on the batting label for information about whether it's best suited for machine or hand quilting, how densely it needs to be quilted so that it won't tear apart during use, how it will shrink, its weight, and its loft, or how fluffy it is. I recommend experimenting with different battings and even combining battings to see what effects you like best. I sometimes use a very thin layer of cotton batting, for weight, along with a low-loft poly batting for fluffiness. This creates a heavier, fuller-looking quilt. I recently began working with wool batting; it's fantastic for both hand and machine quilting, and it has a wonderful drape.

BACKING

The backing can be pieced simply from wide selvage-to-selvage yardage. When piecing large pieces of fabric, I consistently match either the crosswise or lengthwise grains of the material. Piecing large sections of crosswise grain fabric to a section cut on the lengthwise grain can cause puckering. Alternately, you can create a more complex back by using leftover sections of patchwork from the composition on the front and adding other materials from your stash. Make the backing 5" (13 cm) longer and wider than the quilt top.

"I love to quilt. I love to piece on them. I love to wash them. I love to look at pretty quilts. I got to make me another one."

—Lucy T. Pettway, from
The Quilts of Gee's Bend

Basting

The purpose of basting is to hold all the layers securely as you quilt. I baste my quilts before hand quilting, and you will want to baste if you quilt on your home machine. Use blue painter's tape to secure your backing wrong side up to the floor. Layer your batting on top of the backing and cut it to match. Layer your pieced top right side up and center it on top of your batting. Make sure all three layers are smooth from the center out before basting.

I typically baste using 1" to 3" (2.5 cm to 7.5 cm) long running or basting stitches. I start basting in a cross, center top to bottom and center side to side, then diagonally in an *X* through the center of the quilt, and finally all around the edges. Some people pin baste with safety pins or straight pins and some baste in grids. Do what works best for you. Whether basting with stitches or pins, you will remove the basting after the quilting is complete.

Quilting

The term "quilting" refers to the stitching that holds all three layers of your quilt together. Before you get to that step, however, first determine your quilting pattern.

QUILTING PATTERN

The quilting pattern is like a line drawing that is superimposed over the patchwork pattern of your quilt top. When choosing a pattern, consider these variables: Are you machine or hand quilting? How close together do you want your quilting lines? What works in harmony with the patchwork pattern?

The quilting pattern possibilities are infinite. You can stitch in the ditch, which is the term for quilting along the seam lines. You can cross hatch with a diagonal or regular gridded pattern that runs across the entire quilt, or you can free-motion quilt with improvised, unmarked lines.

ECHO QUILTING

My favorite type of quilting pattern is both repetitive and improvisational. I call it echo quilting, and my favorite form for echo quilting is the scallop. Echo quilting patterns can be done by hand or by machine.

ECHO QUILTING

1 Assess the layout of your patchwork and determine a center point or axis line from which you will be echoing out.

2 Chalk a scallop around the edge of the center point and quilt along the chalked line. Or chalk a repeating scallop along one side of the axis and a mirrored but offset scallop on the other side. Quilt along the chalked lines.

3 Quilt from the center out on both sides of the axis by echoing the previously quilted scallop line.

4 Use chalk to refine the arcs of your scallops as needed. If the arcs become too large to echo smoothly, shorten the arc of the scallop and add an additional scallop into the pattern.

5 Continue echoing, adding and subtracting scallops as needed, out to the edge of the quilt.

technique

FINISHING TECHNIQUES

BIG-STITCH HAND QUILTING

1 Position the quilt in the frame so that your hand will be quilting right to left if you are right-handed and left to right if you are left-handed.

2 Thread the needle with a single strand of thread. Don't double it.

3 Make a knot at the end by wrapping the tail around your finger twice, twist and slip thread off, and pull to knot.

4 Pull the knot into the center of the quilt through a seam, from the back side, by inserting the needle ½" (12 mm) away from the starting point. Tug on the thread and manipulate the fabric where the knot is entering to pop the knot into the center of the quilt.

5 Following the line of quilting, slip the tip of your needle through the top of the quilt and through all of the layers. I wear a thimble on my middle finger to push the needle through.

6 Use the middle finger of your secondary hand under the quilt to feel for the needle's point as it pierces through the back of the quilt. Once you feel the needle tip, push it up at a slanted angle through to the top.

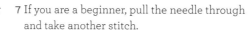

7 If you are a beginner, pull the needle through and take another stitch.

8 As you become more skilled, use a rocking motion to repeat the process until there are several stitches on your needle. Notice how my hand is held in the shape of a C as I rock the needle.

9 Rock the needle in and out, piercing through all layers of your quilt, and focus on making evenly sized and spaced straight stitches. Don't worry about making small stitches. Over time your stitches will naturally become smaller.

10 Once the needle is full of stitches, pull the thread through and begin again.

11 To end the thread, backstitch over your last several stitches. To do this, insert the needle through the top only and bring the needle out where the thread exits the fabric. Push the needle back into the same hole, splitting or catching the thread. Weave the needle in and out between the last stitches on the line.

12 Check to see if the thread is secure by tugging on the last stitch made. When it's secure, pull your needle out and cut the tail of the thread.

QUILTING THE LAYERS

Quilting can be done by machine or by hand. I much prefer the experience and the results of hand quilting. I enjoy the meditative reprieve of hand quilting after an intense session of improvising, and there are benefits to slowing down. When I was younger and hand quilting at public markets, people would come up to me and say, "You are so patient." Of course it wasn't true at the time, but now I am more patient, and some of the credit goes to the hundreds of hours I've spent hand quilting. I like the open dashed line stitch and the subtle texture created by hand quilting. I also like the sense of time and devotion that hand quilting visibly conveys.

I've been hand quilting so long, and am such a beginner at machine quilting, that it actually doesn't take me that much longer to hand quilt. Once you master hand quilting, it will go faster than you think, especially if you use thicker thread and take slightly larger stitches than the old-school benchmark of ten to twelve stitches per inch (2.5 cm).

BIG-STITCH HAND QUILTING

I began using a big stitch to quilt my work in the early 1990s after being exposed to the Japanese tradition of sashiko. Both are basically a running stitch made with thick-weight thread.

I use no. 8 pearl cotton thread with a size 06 embroidery needle, but there are other thread options available in different weights, including actual sashiko thread. Usually I choose a thread color that contrasts with my quilt top, as I like my handwork to stand out. If you are new to hand quilting and don't want your stitches to show, choose a thread color that blends with your quilt top and/or back. The texture created by the hand quilting will still be visible.

I prefer to quilt on a lightweight, collapsible quilting frame constructed from PVC that can be found in most quilt supply shops or online. Some people prefer large oval or circular quilting hoops and others prefer not using a frame at all.

MACHINE QUILTING

The advantages of machine quilting are that it can be done quickly, and the stitches are very sturdy. Linear or channel quilting, in which the lines of quilting run parallel to each other, is best done on a home sewing machine with a walking foot attachment. The home machine can also be used for free-motion quilting, in which the quilting lines can go in any direction, and is done with a free-motion or hopping foot, with the feed dogs lowered. Long-arm quilting machines are great for free-motion quilting larger quilts. Long-arms are also used with repeat pattern guides, called pantagrams, to create a regular pattern across the entire quilt.

Another option for securing the three layers of backing, batting, and top is to hand-tie or "tack," using cotton or wool yarn, string, or embroidery floss. This quick and easy way of finishing is associated with a more utilitarian form of the quilt, the comforter. However, ties can have a stunning visual effect when done creatively.

I prefer to hand-tie with medium-weight wool yarn, the kind that's prone to felting. When washed, the ties felt into cute little doodle balls on the surface of the quilt. Cotton yarn, string, and embroidery floss will felt at the knot over time, but the tails of the ties will remain stringy. Stay away from acrylic, synthetic fibers, and superwash wool. They will not felt, and the ties will loosen over time. When using wool, my needle of choice is a size 18/22 chenille tapestry needle. Experiment with different needles and yarn to find combinations that are easy to thread yet still pull through the quilt without too much effort.

Space the ties from 1" to 10" (2.5 cm to 25 cm) apart according to the density required by the batting. Use a high-loft wool or polyester batting to achieve that puffy comforter look. Here is the way I hand-tied the Rhythmic Grid quilt on page 58.

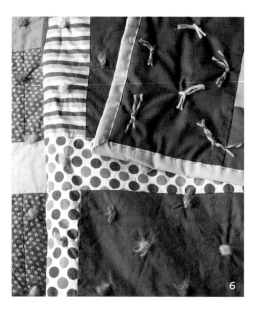

1 Mark along a row at 4" (10 cm) intervals.

2 With a double-threaded needle, take a stitch ¼" to ½" (6 mm to 12 mm) long at each mark, always in the same direction. Continue to mark and stitch rows across the entire quilt. Do not cut the thread.

3 Mark and stitch a second set of rows that run perpendicular and between the previous rows of stitches. Use an alternate wool color if you like.

4 You will now have a grid of lines across the entire surface of your quilt. Snip the yarn at the intersections.

5 Tie off all the stitches using a square knot: right over left, and left over right.

6 Wash and dry the quilt to felt the thread and secure the ties.

technique

Binding

It's time to bind the edges of your quilt, but first there are choices to be made. Factor in both the functional need and the visual effect you are aiming for when choosing a binding. Here are the three binding techniques I most commonly use to finish my quilts.

FOLD-OVER BINDING

A fold-over binding is the simplest and quickest way to bind a quilt. The backing fabric is folded over the top of the quilt and top stitched down. Whatever you've chosen as the backing fabric will be visible on the front.

4

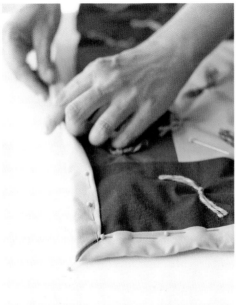

6

8

technique

1 Trim the batting to the size of the quilt top.

2 Decide how wide you want your binding. Trim the backing so it is larger than the trimmed quilt top and batting by double that width on all four sides of the quilt. I typically trim my backing between 1" to 2" (2.5 cm to 5 cm) larger on all sides. It's easy enough to cut the width consistently by eye.

3 Trim the corners at a 45° angle halfway between the point of the backing and the point of the quilt top.

4 Fold the corner over and pin in place.

5 Fold the edges of the backing in half to meet the edge of the quilt top.

6 Fold again over to the top of the quilt and pin in place.

7 Top stitch by machine or by hand with a running stitch through all the layers of the quilt, sewing close to the fold.

8 The corners will self-miter as you fold the binding over the edge. Use a variation of the appliqué stitch (page 150) in the creases of the mitered edges to sew them closed and pull them together.

DOUBLE-FOLD BINDING

A double-fold binding is functional and long-lasting since there are two layers of fabric covering the edge of the quilt. It is sewn onto the front of the quilt and folded over onto the back so it can be seen from the front and the back. I typically make my double-fold binding out of multiple fabrics so that the thin border it creates is visually open.

technique

1 Trim the backing and batting to the same size as the quilt top.

2 Piece a binding strip that is 2½" (6 cm) wide and 10" (25 cm) longer than the perimeter of your quilt, press seams open, then fold the strip in half lengthwise with wrong sides together and press. If you are binding curved edges, make your binding out of bias cut strips.

3 Fold over one short edge of the binding strip by ½" (12 mm) and place this end in the center of one edge of the quilt front, aligning the raw edges with the quilt edge. Beginning 1½" (4 cm) from the end of the strip, sew binding to the quilt with a ¼" (6 mm) seam.

4 Stitch to ¼" (6 mm) from the first corner, secure the stitch, and lift the needle.

5 Fold the binding strip diagonally at a 45° angle and lift it up away from the corner.

6 Fold the binding strip forward vertically at a 90° angle, creasing the top so it is horizontal and in line with the edge of the quilt.

7 Insert the needle and sew a ¼" (6 mm) seam along the next side of the quilt.

8 Continue attaching binding as above, stopping about 3" (7.5 cm) before the starting point.

9 Allowing for an overlap of about 1½" (4 cm), cut off the excess binding and tuck the end of binding into the starting end.

10 Continue stitching right over the join and tie off the stitching securely.

11 Turn the quilt over. Fold the binding over the quilt edge, pin in place, and hand stitch the binding to the back of the quilt with the appliqué stitch (page 150).

12 As you fold and stitch the binding, the corners will self-miter.

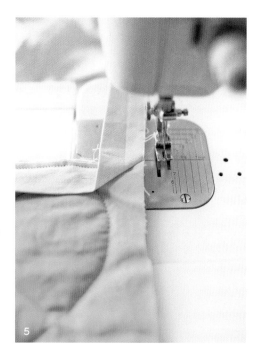

FACING

If you don't want any binding to show on the front of your quilt, use a simple facing to finish your quilt.

2

3

5

1 Create a facing strip as long as the perimeter of your quilt plus 10" (25 cm) from fabric strips 1½" (4 cm) wide. Sew the strips end to end.

2 Sew the facing strip to the top edge of the trimmed quilt top, with right sides facing and taking a ¼" (6 mm) seam. Cut off the excess facing flush with the edge of the quilt top. Sew the facing strip to the bottom edge of the quilt in the same way. Then sew the facing to each side edge of the quilt, pinning or holding the facing seams inward toward the quilt when sewing over the top and bottom facings.

3 At the seam line, finger press the rest of the facing to the back of the quilt, while folding under and pinning in place. As you come to a corner, fold one side down all the way to the edge of the facing and pin.

4 Fold over the adjacent side in the same way so that the folded edge overlaps the previously folded edge.

5 Secure the facing with the appliqué stitch (page 150).

Signing and Labeling

It's a sweet thing to document your quilt on the back. Include your name and the date and other important information like the quilt title, location of where it was made, who it was made for, and the occasion, if it's a gift. Hand embroider the information, making sure not to sew through the front layer of your quilt. Or use a permanent marker, or create a label and appliqué the label to the back.

Making a Hanging Sleeve

A lot of my quilts are made to hang. Some serve double duty: They can be used or hung. Even if your quilts are purely functional, you may need a sleeve so that the quilt can hang in a show.

1 To make a 4" (10 cm) hanging sleeve, cut an 8½" (22 cm) strip of fabric to match the width of the top edge of your quilt top. Turn under the short ends about a ¼" (6 mm) and sew. Sew the long edges wrong sides together to create a tube. Press the tube flat with the seam centered on one side. Do not turn the tube inside out.

2 With the back of your quilt facing up, place and pin the tube, seam side down, in a straight line ¼" to ½" (6 mm to 12 mm) below the top edge of the quilt.

3 If your quilt is slightly irregular, place the sleeve at the lowest point of the edge.

4 Use a running stitch or an appliqué stitch (page 150) to sew the top edge of the tube down, making sure not to pierce your needle through to the front side of your quilt.

5 Once the top edge of the tube is secure, shift the bottom edge of the tube ¼" to ½" (6 mm to 12 mm) above the crease line, so that the top opening of the tube is slightly wider than the bottom being sewn to the quilt. (The bottom side of the tube will be flat but the top side will bubble out slightly to make room for the width of a hanging stick.) Finger press along the bottom edge of the sleeve and pin in place.

6 Sew the pinned bottom edge of the tube in place. Secure the bottom side of the short ends of the tube to the back of the quilt so the hanging stick is easily inserted into the center of the tube and not against the back of the quilt.

5

Quilt Care

I wash my quilts in an oversized front-loading machine on a gentle cycle or by hand in the bathtub using a mild detergent made for washing quilts. Quilts are most vulnerable when wet, so handle with care. Hang or lay flat to dry or machine dry on a low-heat setting.

Resources

Test Quilt Contributors

The following men and women contributed quilts to this book. Stop by the web sites listed here to see more of their amazing work. And see the complete online archive of more than 130 test quilts at daintytime.net.

Emily Cummings, "Sometimes Difficult to See" on page 30, scribblesketch.tumblr.com.

Sarah Fielke, "Hop, Skip and a Jump" on page 110, sarahfielke.com.

Amy Friend, "Scrambled" on page 85, duringquiettime.com.

Penny Gold, "Wild Geese" on page 76, penny-studionotes.blogspot.com.

Robin Cowie Green, "Sidestep" on page 69, instagram.com/fernstitch.

Susannah Heath, "Polar Vortex" on page 76, fiberchic.blogspot.com.

Veronica Hofman-Ortega, "Guitar Strings Improv" on page 38, fiberanticsbyveronica.com.

Rossie Hutchinson, "A Dance for Emily" on page 68, r0ssie.blogspot.com.

Mina Kennison, "Burning Love" on page 77, kindaquilty.blogspot.com.

Heather Kojan, "Surf" on page 110, heatherkojan.blogspot.com.

Beth Lehman, "untitled" on page 39, yellowhousedays.blogspot.com.

Michelle McLatchy, "Against The Grain" on page 30, eclecticgnome.blogspot.ca.

Barb Mortell, "Stacks in Red and Yellow" on page 38, houseofbug.blogspot.ca.

Ashley Newcomb, "Pocho Dots & Squares" on page 31, filminthefridge.com.

Sharon O'Brien, "you are here" on page 56, ravelry.com/designers/sharon-obrien.

Pamela Rocco, "Rhythmic Grid" on page 68, phone: 831.713.5487

Latifah Saafir, "Indigo Bloom" on page 94, thequiltengineer.com.

Stacey Sharman, "Northwest" on page 111, peppermintpinwheels.com.

Marion Shimoda, "Bias Petal Play" on page 95, mshimoda.blogspot.com.

Drew Steinbrecher, "Letting Go" on page 102, andrewsteinbrecher.com.

Lucie Summers, "curve" on page 57, summersville.etsy.com.

Carolyn Wong, "Beginning of the Universe" on page 103, instagram.com/cwong619.

East Bay Modern Quilt Guild, round robin quilts on pages 48–49, eastbaymodernquiltguild.wordpress.com.

SHERRI LYNN WOOD ONLINE

daintytime.net

instagram.com/daintytime

facebook.com/daintytime.net

facebook.com/groups/daintytime.improv.
handbook

twitter.com/daintytime

flickr.com/photos/sherriwood

Quilting Reference

Accidentally on Purpose: The Aesthetic Management of Irregularities in African Textiles and African-American Quilts by Eli Leon
(Figge Art Museum, 2007)

Anna Williams: Her Quilts & Their Influences by Katherine Watts
(American Quilter's Society, 1995)

A Communion of the Spirits: African-Amercian Quilters, Preservers, and Their Stories by Roland L. Freeman
(Thomas Nelson, 1996)

Crossroads: Constructions, Markings, and Structures by Nancy Crow
(Breckling Press, 2008)

Let it Shine: Improvisation in African-American Star Quilts by Eli Leon
(William D. Cannon Art Gallery, 2001)

Nancy Crow: Work in Transition by Nancy Crow
(American Quilter's Society, 1992)

The Quilts of Gee's Bend by William Arnett, Alvia Wardlaw, Jane Livingston, and John Beardsley
(Tinwood Books, 2002)

Signs and Symbols: African Images in African American Quilts by Maude Southwell Wahlman
(Museum of American Folk Art, Penguin, 1993)

Unconventional & Unexpected: American Quilts Below the Radar by Roderick Kiracofe
(STC Craft/Abrams, 2014)

Who'd a Thought It: Improvisation in African-American Quiltmaking by Eli Leon
(San Francisco Craft and Folk Art Museum, 1987)

"I'm going to be up to something real dangerous when I get through with this. This quilt done killed two people."

—Arbie Williams, from *Let It Shine: Improvisation in African-American Star Quilts* by Eli Leon

Other Reference

The Art and Heart of Drum Circles
by Christine Stevens
(Hal Leonard, 2003)

Bossypants by Tina Fey
(Little Stranger, Inc., Reagan Arthur
Books, 2011)

How Music Works by David Byrne
(McSweeney's, 2012)

*I Ching: Walking Your Path,
Creating Your Future* by Hilary Barrett
(Acturus, 2010)

*Improv Wisdom: Don't Prepare,
Just Show Up* by Patricia Ryan Madison
(Bell Tower Press, 2005)

*Radical Acceptance: Embracing Your Life
with the Heart of a Buddha* by Tara Brach
(Bantam Dell, 2003)

Systems-Centered Therapy for Groups
by Yvonne M. Agazarian
(Karnac Books, 2004)

*Truth in Comedy: The Manual of
Improvisation* by Charna Halpern, Del
Close, and Kim "Howard" Johnson
(Meriwether Pub, 1994)

Zen Mind, Beginner's Mind
by Shunryu Suzuki
(Shambhala, 2011)

Sources

SUE FOX
Fox Dreams Quilting & Design
(long-arm quilting)
2625 8th St. Berkeley, CA 94710
510-849-0908

AURIFIL THREAD
Machine quilting thread
aurifil.com

FAIRFIELD
Wool batting
fairfieldworld.com

LACIS
Hand quilting thread, needles, and
thimbles
lacis.com

Design Considerations and Mind Tools

Acknowledgments

The day I turned in this manuscript to the publisher an overwhelming feeling of gratitude rushed to meet the occasion of its completion.

I thought first of my teachers: Eli Leon; Nancy Crow, who told me more than twenty years ago that I could cut and piece a quilt without a ruler; the great African-American quilts by Rosie Lee Tomkins, Angie Tobias, Arbie Williams, Maple Swift, Laverne Brackens, Sherry Byrd, Marzella Tatum, Anna Williams, the quilters of Gee's Bend, and of many others. Dr. Norma Safransky, who taught me to harness the creative energy of emotion by introducing me to the practical mind tools of Systems-Centered Therapy. And the teachers and my fellow students at Pan Theater.

My friends: Michele, Michael, Jeff, Hector, Dan, Alison, Mary, Jimmy, Roland, and many more, who reminded me that, even in the midst of creative solitude, I belong; Bret for listening patiently as I worked through my insecurities; Freddy Freckles, a canine bundle of energy, who kept me on my toes and laughing.

My father, brother, and sister, for supporting my creative life even though my path has been very different from theirs; my nieces and nephews just for existing and being a part of our loving family. And in memory of my dynamic mother, Linda Sue, who would have been so proud.

My colleagues: Paul, Sylvia, Sanford, Leesy, and Peggy at St. Gregory of Nyssa Episcopal Church. In contrast to the intensity of writing this book, going to my "day job" was a holiday; special thanks to Sara Miles, for helping me clarify my voice as my unofficial line editor.

The great collaborative project of writing a book is a blessing in itself, but even more so when working with such a talented team of professionals. Not only does the beauty of Sara Remington's photographs speak to her talent, commitment, and professionalism, she and her staff were great fun to work with.

Christine Doyle, as the technical editor, had both the logical and creative mindset to understand that I was writing a different kind of craft book.

Book designer Sarah Gifford shaped the abundant raw materials with a cheerful, open ear, into something beautiful, embodied, and whole.

For Melanie Falick, my editor, I have nothing but praise. She took a great risk and made a great investment in this project. I appreciate our honest exchanges and the creative freedom she gave me to pursue my vision. She kept me steady.

Of course I am incredibly thankful for my agent Joy Tutela, who believed in my voice and got this whole ball rolling. She continues to be my champion.

I am grateful for the growing community of quilt makers, the readers of my blog, and for the 230 talented quilt makers who signed up to test the project scores in advance. Their feedback significantly influenced this book's content. The test quilts not published in this book can be viewed online at daintytime.net.

Special thanks to the East Bay Modern Quilters and to Stacey Sharman, for organizing the Improv Round Robin photographed on pages 44–49, and to all the participants in the workshop. Sue Fox did a lovely job machine quilting the quilts for the Strings (page 32), Patchwork Doodle (page 50), and Layered Curve (page 78) scores. And to my very capable and talented intern Lukaza Branfman-Verissimo.

Thanks to both Aurifil, for providing luminous thread, and to Fairfield, for providing the most amazing wool batting. Both products were a delight to work with.

Finally, I am deeply grateful to the Joan Mitchell Foundation, whose generous grant gave me the financial freedom to embark on this two-year endeavor worry free.

for my sister, jennifer kathleen,
and for all my quilt-loving sisters and brothers

Published in 2015 by Stewart, Tabori & Chang
An imprint of ABRAMS

Text and illustrations © 2015 Sherri Lynn Wood
Photographs © 2015 Sara Remington unless otherwise noted.
Photographs on pages 29, 36–37, 54–55, 64–65, 74–75, 82–83, 91, 101, 108–109 © 2015 Sherri Lynn Wood

Library of Congress Control Number: 2014942998
ISBN: 978-1-61769-138-6

Editor: Melanie Falick and Christine Doyle
Designer: Sarah Gifford
Production Manager: True Sims

The text of this book was composed in Archer, Bryant, and French Script.

Printed and bound in The United States
10 9 8 7 6 5 4 3 2 1

Stewart, Tabori & Chang books are available at special discounts when purchased in quantity for
premiums and promotions as well as fundraising or educational use. Special editions can also be
created to specification. For details, contact specialsales@abramsbooks.com or the address below.

THE ART OF BOOKS SINCE 1949
115 West 18th Street
New York, NY 10011
www.abramsbooks.com